REPORTS FROM THE PRESENT

by the same author

INTIMATE VOICES: SELECTED WORK 1965–83

RADICAL RENFREW

PLACES OF THE MIND:
THE LIFE AND WORK OF JAMES THOMSON ('B.V.')

REPORTS FROM THE PRESENT
Selected Work
1982–94

TOM LEONARD

JONATHAN CAPE
LONDON

First published 1995

1 3 5 7 9 10 8 6 4 2

© Tom Leonard 1995

Tom Leonard has asserted his right
under the Copyright, Designs and Patents Act, 1988
to be identified as the author of this work

First published in the United Kingdom in 1995 by
Jonathan Cape
Random House, 20 Vauxhall Bridge Road, London SW1V 2SA

Random House Australia (Pty) Limited
20 Alfred Street, Milsons Point, Sydney,
New South Wales 2061, Australia

Random House New Zealand Limited
18 Poland Road, Glenfield,
Auckland 10, New Zealand

Random House South Africa (Pty) Limited
PO Box 337, Bergvlei, South Africa

Random House UK Limited Reg. No. 954009

A CIP catalogue record for this book
is available from the British Library

Papers used by Random House UK Limited are natural,
recyclable products made from wood grown in sustainable forests.
The manufacturing processes conform to the environmental
regulations of the country of origin.

ISBN 0–224–03169–4

Printed in Great Britain by
Mackays of Chatham PLC

for
PETE HODGKISS
editor & publisher

Not Poetry 1980–85
Poetry Information 1970–80
GALLOPING DOG PRESS 1976–91

This book is in two parts: *Reports from the Present,* and *Antidotes Anecdotes and Accusations.*

Reports from the Present is a sequence of poetry and prose written over the last ten years, and separately published in different forms.

Antidotes Anecdotes and Accusations is a selection of other, mainly satirical work, written and performed or published during the same period.

I thank Black Sparrow Press for permission to quote from the poetry of Charles Reznikoff; and Jerome Rothenberg for permission to quote his words in interview.

TL

CONTENTS

Reports from the Present: Selected Poems and Prose 1984–94

Several of these pieces were written for or were first placed in the *Edinburgh Review*. The opening and closing poetry sequences were published as booklets by Galloping Dog Press, Newcastle. "The Present Tense" appeared in the Hull University magazine, *Bête Noire*, in Spring 1991.

"Literature, Dialogue, Democracy" is a slightly abridged version of my introduction to the anthology *Radical Renfrew: Poetry from the French Revolution to the First World War*, published by Polygon in 1990. The essay "On Reclaiming the Local" was written during the compilation of that anthology, and refers to it.

"Poetry, Schools, Place" was written for the magazine *Teaching English* in response to a request to write something about the teaching of poetry in schools.

The essay and catechism "On the Mass Bombing of Iraq and Kuwait" was published by AK Press, Stirling, in 1991.

Situations Theoretical
and Contemporary

somewhere between stocks & shares
and the "commonsensical" editorial

pity the poor arts page
thinking itself alone

The schooner *The Mother of Parliaments* has
    anchored in the bay.
The first British ship has reached your land.

See the row-boat, pulling to the shore.
See the ballot-boxes, glinting in the sun!

Run and tell your fellow-tribesmen.
We are going to have a referendum!
Shall we join the British Empire?

Today is National Income Card-Carrying Day.
On this day all citizens must wear cards prominently
   declaring their total income from all sources for the
   previous twelve months.

How full the underground shelters are this morning.
All those advocates of "tighter control of the money supply".
And there is that expert on "international terrorism".
Quite a card, eh?

Quick though – there goes the Chancellor of the Exchequer.
Oh dear. No pep-talk today!

You are tracing the link between existential angst and male
    sexual guilt.
From the consciousness of guilt to the guilt of consciousness.
From Dostoevsky to Sartre.

Your audience this morning is from the "Third World".
Their bodies are skeletal.
Their eyes seem very large.

One approaches the rostrum.
Food. Food.

Dear Member: The Party for the Political Advancement of the Upwardly Mobile Sons and Daughters of Parents who were Working Class

again requests five dead metaphors and five banal alliterations for inclusion in our party leader's keynote speech to forthcoming annual party conference

four acceptances again guarantee admission to conference, with the opportunity to participate in the ten-minute standing ovation at the end of the speech itself.

Last year's poll-toppers, "The demise of the dreary dogmatist" and "A return to radical realism", remain eligible.

Bon appetit!

You have returned to Glasgow after a long exile.
A *Glasgow Herald* special edition is selling like hot cakes.
It publishes a Turkish poet's abstruse new song.

This Turkish poet is of an international cast of mind.
He also has an unselfconscious enjoyment of working-class
    culture.
In fact his song is about a match between Glasgow Celtic
    and Glasgow Rangers.

A certain Professor MacFadyen has detected the influence
    of MacDiarmid.

as I was waiting upon a bus in Byres Road
musing upon the *echtness* of the glasgow cultural renaissance

an elderly gentleman came walking by with a smile
who bid good morning to a woman of slightly more tender
  years
who smiled in reply and said

and how is the wee dog this morning mister mackay

It is five years since the edict "Only the trauchle is clean".

Now the Inspector of Literature himself has sent his *Collected Trauchles* for review.

Grimly but morally refreshed you reach page five-hundred-and-eighty-three.

"There is not a spark of humour throughout this wholly admirable book," you begin your review.

"Nor has irony caused its customary obfuscation through bad faith."

The administrative resource base of school focused projects and the college-initiated curriculum in the field provides in-service whole-school comprehensive packages for the formulation, implementation and evaluation of major new initiatives developed within the time constraints appropriate to areas of deprivation. The new multi-purpose role of language across the curriculum will promote the acquisition of subject-specific concepts designed to support and under-pin the implementation participation and development of supportive group structures relevant to the mutual inter-change of the specific school situation in the context of the community. The conceptual structure of investigative skills will be developed in relation to the creation of dynamic self-initiated visits to explore, redefine and extend criterion-referenced modules for individual problem-solving processes. This should facilitate the co-ordination and liaison of relevant core teams in providing an impetus to integrate in-service evaluation as part of the monitoring and review of inter-dependent consultancy approaches on a one-to-one basis.

The coach-driver makes an announcement.
"Your poems should have one of two titles:
'The Vanity of Human Wishes', or 'There But for the Grace
   of God'."

The passengers are excited.
Who will win the word processor? Will it be me?
The lights turn to green. The bus moves off at last.

Let the tour of the slums begin!

We have decided to make Scotland secure.
This is strategically essential.
No question.

Scottish people have nothing to fear.
Noise pollution should not be a problem.
And all construction work will be landscaped.

We have decided to make America secure.
This is strategically essential.
No question.

Scottish people have nothing to fear.
Noise pollution should not be a problem.
And all construction work will be landscaped.

Scotland has become an independent socialist republic.
At last.

Eh?
You pinch yourself.
Jesus Christ. You've slept in again.

And their judges spoke with one dialect,
but the condemned spoke with many voices.

And the prisons were full of many voices,
but never the dialect of the judges.

And the judges said:
"No-one is above the Law."

Poetry, Schools, Place

I was once asked to visit a school to give advice on the writing of poetry to some pupils taking the sixth-year "creative writing" option. I told them that in my opinion creative writing had nothing to do with schools; that because educational institutions took to do with creative literature this did not mean that literature had, or should have, anything to do with educational institutions. This last sentence I repeated, as it pointed to a distinction that has become blurred in many people's minds, who think that the highest acclaim a writer can expect is to be "set" – as they say of concrete – in an examination; nor is it a distinction that some teachers seemed keen to accept.

The advice I gave was this: since all subjects in schools are exam-centred, then the first thing to do with the "creative-writing" course, as with any other, is to go to the past papers, to see what the anonymous examiners want. I had had a look at some of the past papers myself, in my preparations for my visit to the school. It seemed that what was required was a poem in the style of an established twentieth-century Scottish poet – e.g. MacCaig, Morgan, MacDiarmid in Scots; this poem should be on a theme of the type usually asked for each year; and the poem should be written from a generally liberal-Christian point of view – at any rate some previous questions had seemed to assume this as the standpoint of the person sitting the exam.

The pupils should compose such a poem as soon as possible at the start of their course, learn it by heart, and dump it down when it came to the big day. The idea of actually writing a poem "under exam conditions" was an obscenity, an absurdity, and the whole idea had more to do with how certain educationalists fancied one should regard the status of literature in schools than it had to do with the reality of the creative process – or anything else. By even considering it possible to create poetry in an exam, the pupils would be insulting Art, insulting their own existence – and all to flatter some anonymous people who thought that in their own quiet, modest way they were perhaps just carrying out the next logical step in the management of the course of Literature.

I was trying to be practical though, not simply dismissive. Having got their "exam poem" out the road, pupils could spend the main part of the course time actually trying to do some serious writing. Whether or not they could physically do the writing in a classroom, nonetheless the weekly setting aside of time for writing could be a good stimulus and discipline. If the writing was done at home, then the time at school could be used to hold writers' group discussions (the chairperson's role being in rotation) assuming enough were doing the course to form a group. The extent of the teacher's involvement, if any, would depend on individual circumstances. Some teachers might be a help, others could be an impediment. If the pupils were serious about writing, they had to realise that they themselves were in control: if need be the writers' group should take a vote on whether or not the teacher be made welcome to attend.

But besides meaning teaching people how to write poetry, the phrase "teaching poetry" can mean teaching people to read it, and teaching them what you think is worth reading. I've already written elsewhere (e.g. in "The Proof of the Mince Pie", *Intimate Voices*, Vintage, 1995) that I see "English Literature" exams in schools and universities as central anti-creative rites in which Art is turned into property and students compelled to be witnessed in an act of acquisition. The property derived from the work of art is sold as a commodity to the examiner, who places a value on it and ultimately offers in return a bill of currency. The devaluation suffered by this currency in times of high unemployment does not alter the principles on which the exchange has taken place. This is not to mention either the effect the exams have in deciding the range of poetry that is held to be "serious", i.e. that which is most suited to examination marking. A "real" poem is one which can be seen as a kind of treasure chest of valuables, which the student should remove one by one and display to the examiner. Most valuables are wrapped in "figures of speech". Those traditions of poetry that have abandoned this way of composition since before the First World War, tend to be treated as "marginal". One reason is because examiners haven't yet worked out a gradeable vocabulary of criticism.

So far, so negative – though it's what I believe, in these aspects. Yet all I am trying to articulate, here as in other essays, is how the philosophic basis of the system of teaching Literature within schools and universities cannot but reflect the philosophic basis of the society of which these institutions are a part. That basis of our society, is:

$$object = property = commmodity$$

which is extended to include:

$$human = object = property = commodity$$

which, by the way, is the "reasoning" behind the current mass closures planned in Strathclyde.

What Art offers as refutation of this last equation, through and in a work of art, is:

$$human = object = human$$

by which I mean the relationship between writer writing and reader reading.

23

What I'm talking about, then, is Art as Encounter. But the teaching of Literature as I have experienced it consists of the teaching of a theology of encounter by which people are rewarded according to their ability to speak convincingly of a personal encounter that has not usually taken place. It has not usually taken place because such an encounter can only occur where the self has the freedom not to have this encounter if it doesn't want to, and not to speak of this encounter if it actually has occurred. There are generations of people who have been reared to think that Art is something that exists in order that people might pour torrents of critical opinion over one another, and that the person who is reduced to silence by the presence of a work of art is either an ignoramus or a fool. But the first right that ought to be maintained in the presence of a work of art is the right to silence, though this right to silence is precisely what the present educational system attempts to reject. A "candidate" of course though still does have the right to be silent if he or she so chooses: after all, a person can choose to have Nothing Out Of Ten, which is the going rate for silence on the educational free market. But the most worthwhile criticism that I have listened to has always come from someone who has felt the necessity, after a while, retrospectively to examine the nature of the silence to which they have been reduced.

I grew up in Pollok, a housing-scheme in the south-west of Glasgow. It was just a housing-scheme to me, in other words a mass of houses without history that had been constructed mostly after the war. Being of the Catholic tribe, I daily passed safely through three miles of Protestants and other non-Catholics on my way to Cardonald, where was to be found the nearest Catholic Secondary. I spent all my leisure time either exclusively with these tribal friends, or else on my own, doing such things as following the lemonade and beer bottles down the River Levern stream, throwing stones at them until I could record that another German U-boat had been sunk. But I have children of my own now, and I'm no longer interested in the minutiae of my own childhood. What I am interested in is the childhood of the place that I had my childhood in; I feel that the more I know of that then the more concretely I will understand the society my own children are now inheriting. It can be easy to be pessimistic, seeing thousands upon thousands of children growing up in a society where to be under 25 years of age seems increasingly to be regarded as some kind of social crime; a society swamped with goods produced by cheap labour overseas, imported through non-union cheap-labour merchant ships, sold in high street shops – whose profits have never been larger – by cheap-labour young people on what is called "training schemes"; sold to customers, many of them unemployed, through credit schemes financed from the profits the companies are making. Human equals object equals property equals commodity.

No other water in Scotland of anything like equal dimensions, we verily believe, contributes nearly so much to the manufacturing prosperity of the country, as does the Levern in its short course of some six or seven miles. A sadly tortured streamlet it is, in truth. What with dams, and lades, mill-wheels and colouring matters of every hue, with which its bosom is fretted and stained at every turn, it has really a pitiable common-sewer aspect by the time it gets sneaking into the Cart beyond Crookston. Its pollution, however, is associated with the prosperity of the Barrhead people. Their printfields, factories, and bleachfields, are dependent on its originally pellucid waters, and without them their "decline and fall" would speedily be consummated. Long, therefore, may it continue a willing and useful drudge! Lackadaisical poets may whine over the decay of sentiment, and puling painters maunder about the destruction of the beautiful; but to our mind the most interesting of streams is that on the banks of which exists an industrious, a comfortable, and an intelligent population.

So writes Hugh MacDonald, in his *Rambles Round Glasgow* of 1854. Peter MacArthur's "Levern Water Revisited" from his *Musings in Minstrelsy* (1880) seems to be the type of "whining" MacDonald had in mind:

> All now seems changed; yon pearly clouds, high on their azure way,
> Look dimmer now, and yon far hills seem veil'd in darker grey;
> The cottage where my fathers dwelt – "the auld thack house"– is gone;
> Where round my mother's feet I play'd there's no remaining stone;
> Gone are the bow'rs where Age repos'd; or Youth, with whisp'ring tale,
> Sat, when the gloamin' hours were past, beneath the star-light pale,
> > Though still with chiding wail,
> > The Levern winds by brake, and loan,
> > And fills my ear with sorrowing moan.

But all literature is evidence and information. Who were MacArthur's models? When did printed poems first arrive in Pollok? Who had the first libraries? Who had access to them? Which of the animals and plants mentioned in poems are still there? What did the poets do for a living? What did the land look like before all the council houses were built? Who didn't have leisure to write?

I think that poetry should be used as a source of material information, and the aesthetic experience be left private to the individual. I think that people should be given the confidence and the means to construct their own place in the history of the world and its literature, setting out from what is within sight and touch of their own physical being. I would like it if teachers in schools were somehow taught, or were required to find out, the application of their particular discipline to the particular locality in which they teach. I mean that the school should be in fact a centre of local learning and information about the ground on which teachers and pupils walk, what was on it before the school and the surrounding houses were built, and what the people in that particular locality did, wrote, and made as far back as the history of that locality can be traced. It's from what people see, hear and touch, from where they physically are that the educational process should begin, from where people can be "led out" – and given the means to choose their own history. Without this, I think a person's sense of history may be restricted to an isolated Story of their Own Childhood, and passivity and a mythology of inevitability about societal change be the result.

I want schools to get away from the idea of literature as a reservoir of "characters" from whom "we" derive "our" sense of moral values and knowledge of Life: this assumes that the moral values, and the knowledge of Life, is such as has already been discovered by the teacher and the anonymous body of examiners. It assumes a fixed core of values which the literature is thought to exemplify, and a fixed core of knowledge at which teacher and examiner have safely arrived. This kind of complacency leads for instance to the blanket pre-eminence given to George Orwell in the literature curriculum in schools, even in classes where very few novels are read. I believe his centrality is as a powerful maker of frightening allegories that are generally used to teach young people What Our Society Is Not, i.e. "what the other half of the world is". Only by recognising how many thousands of children each year receive this message can one begin to ask whether the societies depicted by Orwell are in such striking antithesis to our own.

*

A boy is walking by the banks of the Levern. He remembers that a book he was reading says the origin of the word was in "Levernani", a Pictish tribe. There's been some argument about that though. How long after the Ice Age would that be? Pollok was full of those drumlin things when you looked around: the hill up Leithland Road down past the chapel, the hill at the back of the school, the hill over the Green Bridge at Braidcraft Road.

He looked left from the Green Bridge to the tower that was all that was left of Crookston Castle. Of course Mary Queen of Scots couldn't have seen the Battle of Langside from there as Scott had her do; but she'd have been able to see up past Househillwood alright, where that Covenanter was killed. The boy's grandparents wouldn't have known about him, since they'd been brought up Catholics. How horrible it was the way people in the twentieth century had hugged their tribal histories to themselves. No wonder they had never been able to unite, and them on the same land.

He thought of Tannahill's poem to Crookston Castle. Over beyond the Castle around Paisley Road West would be where Hogg and Tannahill parted company shortly before Tannahill killed himself. The boy turned away and looked down Brockburn Road past the roundabout.

Beyond the woods on the left was Pollok House. When was it exactly that the Maxwells first got the land, and why? He wanted to check it out. For a long time theirs must have been the biggest library in the district. The people who were able to visit too, like that religious writer Thomas Erskine of Linlathen – who had influenced Coleridge the poet, his father had told him.

Of course there were the people who wouldn't have got using the library at all. The boy thought of his favourite local poet, David Wingate of Cowglen, going down the mines when he was nine, less than a mile from where Maxwell's house and library was located. It was Wingate who wrote the poems about letting children have a day in the country, because they needed the fresh air away from their work. At least now there were none of Maxwell's gamekeepers to disturb the boy's walk.

> In the whinny slopes o' Cathkin
>   Or on Pollok's woody knowes
> He already roams in fancy
>   Where he kens the haw-tree grows.
> On the bitter blast that's brewin'
>   He looks West wi' hopefu' ee,
> For he kens the woods frae keepers
>   In sic weather will be free.

It was good to read poetry out loud. Your voice was a good thing, wherever you came from. He had enjoyed reading out Dunbar and Gavin Douglas the week before. He knew that although he couldn't understand the words at first, he had been able to say the sounds very easily once he had had a few things explained; words might have gone, but the sounds had still been passed by word of mouth over five hundred years. "Never mind stopping to get every word," his teacher had said to him, "if you like it enough you'll want to find out what it means."

That was the teacher he had seen looking upset sitting reading a book. The boy had meant to sneak away unnoticed, but the teacher had called him back. "I'm not ashamed to be found upset reading a book," he'd said, "and I hope you never will be either." He told the boy he was reading Shakespeare's The Winter's Tale, and the bit that always overcame him was the bit where Leontes's wife, as a statue, comes back to life. The play was about a man who was jealous when he had no reason to be, who treated his wife as an object and, in the last act, she appears on the stage as one – a statue. But then the man saw the difference between an object and a human being, and he saw what a unique human being his wife had been, and how he wished she was only alive again. And then the statue moved.

In a way it was a story about a really basic thing, about how you can wish that someone you loved who has died could only come back for five minutes, if only to tell them that you're sorry for something you did while they were alive. But at a deeper level it was one of Shakespeare's great statements about Art, that he knows he's doing this for you, he knows that you know it, and what he's saying is that Art is so precious because only in it can an object come to have human life in your presence.

On Reclaiming the Local

or

The Theory of the Magic
Thing

The "Glasgow operative" is, while trade is good and wages high, the quietest and most inoffensive of creatures. He cares comparatively little for the affairs of the nation, he is industrious and contented. Each six months he holds a saturnalia – one on New Year's Day, the other at the Fair (occurring in July) and his excesses at these points keep him poor during the intervals. During periods of commercial depression, however, when wages are low, and he works three-quarter time, he has a fine nose to scent political iniquities. He begins to suspect that all is not right with the British constitution. These unhappy times, too, produce impudent demagogues, whose power of lungs and floods of flashy rhetoric work incredible mischief. To these he seriously inclines his ear. He is hungry and excited. He is more anxious to reform Parliament than to reform himself. He cries out against tyranny of class-legislation, forgetting the far harder tyranny of the gin-palace and the pawn-shop.

(Alexander Smith, *A Summer in Skye*, Ch. 16, 1865)

This passage could have been called "The Problem of Them". And so many urban poems, pieces of prose, and whole anthologies of either or both, have been produced for which "The Problem of Them" would have been the most honest title. The works assume that those supposedly described don't read the literature that supposedly describes them. Smith here assumes that "the" Glasgow operative will never be the reader: the operative is a predictable behaviour pattern, which pattern does not include reading the works of Alexander Smith. "An" operative would have a behaviour pattern. "The" operative is one. Readers of R. D. Laing might recognise the strategy. In a sense "the Glasgow operative" is the Patient, while the writer has become the Doctor, the man-who-sees, the benign possessor of superior insight: in other words, a traditional image of the Poet.

This patriarchal image of the poet as detached diagnostic judge still dominates influential literary scenes. Most of Morrison and Motion's *The Penguin Book of Contemporary British Poetry*, for instance, is relentlessly judgmental. Separation is assumed – of the judging from the personal experience, of the poet/narrator from the beings who inhabit the world described. This is what is expected, this is what being a Real Poet is all about. The poet is a spectator at someone else's experience, be that someone else a he, a she, "they", or the I of former(!) working-class days. This is to be "objective", the professional tone, the invisible suit of office. The "professional" exists through a language that acquits him of present personal involvement; he is in control, through his craft. The ardently opinionated, the ardent in all forms, the raisers of voices, the thumpers on the table, the "swearers", the passionate, those who burst into tears – these are all absent. This would be unprofessional, "emotionalist", "uncraftsmanlike". To return to the Laingian reference, this would all indicate the presence of a Patient: and this is an anthology of Doctors.

Now you can range through nineteenth-century literary criticism into the twentieth, from the introduction to the *Lyrical Ballads*, Coleridge via Germany, Arnold, Browning, Ruskin, Carlyle right through until you eventually arrive in the room that Mr Eliot is sorting out his objective correlative in, and had you lived through the period in question, and had had an attentive ear, you would have noticed as time progressed that the voices around you discussing the books you were reading, seemed to sound more and more sort of, ehm, "objective". The trouble was that after Wordsworth had been rrolled in Earrth's diurrnial urrn, and education was getting a bit universalised, the chaps hit on this super wheeze, namely how to turn your own voice into an object of social status. Nothing sinister, nothing undemocratic. All you needed to acquire this property yourself, was a fair bit of money. But if your own voice became an object that you shared in common with other fellows who happened also to have a fair bit of money, how could this voice, as object, be other than objective? Now, when you opened your mouth, you had the power to be im-personal.

*　　　　　　　*　　　　　　　*

William Elder (First Supervisor of the Fountain Gardens, Paisley): from *To the Defenders of Things as They Are* (1870)

Why speak of peace, of order, and of law?
Teach mute subserviency to those who draw
The water, hew the wood, and dig the soil,
Whose piteous fate is hard incessant toil?
On land and sea, to work from day to day,
To heap up wealth, but which they may
Ne'er hope to share with those who rule
Their fate, and who in church and school
Teach obedience passive, doctrine fit for slaves.
To make men bow to tyrants, priests, and knaves,
Oh! when will mankind cease to heed such teachers?
Send to the "right about" the glib and oily preachers
Of such a gospel, who, in the past as now,
Have taught the people 'twas their fate to bow
And be content and happy in that station,
Where "God has placed them" to enrich the nation,
To work for kings, aristocrats, and priests so vile,
Who live at ease upon the "holy" spoil
They wring from labour, and who feed and gorge
Revel in pomp, while others toil in mine and forge.

*　　　　　　　*　　　　　　　*

The trouble with asking humans to enact the impersonal is that they usually do so by objectifying the humans around

35

them. The humans around them won't behave like objects, so the "impersonal" diagnostician has to construct mechanistic models of those humans that turn them into the objects they have refused to become. The models of depersonalisation are inevitably linguistic, and thus at the heart of politics is language, at the heart of language is politics. Always the converse happens to what is supposed to be going on. An address to a city-as-person, as for instance, Alexander Smith's address to "Glasgow" in his best-known poem of that name, anthropomorphises beyond the personal conflict on which urban trade is actually based, to a single "personal" unity which can be seen as "natural" or aesthetically invigorating. The anthropomorphic functionalist image serves to create a bogus unified "personality": it does so by leaving the streets clear of those whose opinions, if actually listened to, might spoil the image of a healthy and unified "body" politic.

In Britain the dominant literary tradition still "taught" in educational institutions has been established by clearing the streets in this manner. A dominant value-system has been allowed to marginalise that which does not correspond to it, declaring it deviant and therefore invalid. It has been able to do so by the method of making the mode of expression of these dominant values literally synonymous with "objectivity". It is the mode of expression that counts: that device by which the persona is given the status of being detached, impersonal, above the battle. In speech it has been achieved through the fee-paying Received Pronunciation, buttressed by the Classics-based prescriptive grammar hammered into the pupils. These are the schools where, every one of them, the British Army has its Officer Cadet Corps, where the young Inheritors of Objective Speech take first steps in that training to lead into future battle those ordinary citizens trapped in the expression of their own personal language.

Since the "leaders" are separate from their language, a piece of purchased property held in common amongst themselves, when they address you, their being stands at a tangent to what they have expressed. When one as an outsider attempts dialogue, one addresses not simply a person but a closed system of value, which stands between the two human beings in attempted communication. To speak back when addressed, one must attempt first of all to digest all the components of that system of value oneself, in order that one can oneself stand at a tangent, and reply to the person who has addressed you, from within that closed system of value that is given. In so doing, one will of course have enlarged that closed system slightly, by the addition of one's own contribution, while one exists personally unchanged outside it. And all the components of that value-system will have been fractionally altered, too, by the addition of one's own contribution. This, of course, is the Theory of the Magic Thing.

*   *   *

Marion Bernstein: from *Mirren's Musings* (1876)

Human Rights

Man holds so exquisitively tight
To everything he deems his right;
If woman wants a share, to fight
She has, and strive with all her might.

But we are nothing like so jealous
As any of you surly fellows;
Give us our rights and we'll not care
To cheat our brothers of their share.

Above such selfish, *man-like* fright,
We'd give fair play, let come what might,
To he or she folk, black or white,
And haste the reign of Human Right.

*   *   *

Like speech, like literature. Here the writer will be detached, at a tangent to the work produced, and the Magic Thing will be buried in the work itself. This Magic Thing will seem like an ordinary thing to the personae created by the man-who-sees, but to the reader-who-knows, this seemingly ordinary thing will in fact stand out as an inner Magic Thing, that places a value on the actions of those described. This value can be seen as the profit-value from the outlay on the personae created. As such, one might think that the personae have only been created in order that some profit-value might be reaped from them. From a functionalist point of view though what's important is that the profits reaped in any society from such transactions are not in a currency that might destabilise the prevailing monetary system. Hence the two basic functions of the application of the Theory of the Magic Thing are:

1. verification of a closed value-system
2. control of the money supply

This is a restatement of the opening criticism of Smith's "Glasgow". Part of the verification of the closed value-system must consist in indicating that the lower orders don't have access to it. Classical music, literature, philosophy; a narrator couldn't casually mention, without comment about conflict, that a working-class person happened to be listening to Beethoven. That is one of the things that the working class "don't do". The narrator would have to bring in some Magic Thing to cure the supposed conflict within the work, or, more likely, let the Beethoven stand as the Magic Thing that showed why the narrator couldn't go back to his poignant old roots. (I think some of Tony Harrison's work does this very clearly.) The truth is that having nodded through the value-system, it's almost impossible for the narrator not to sound either patronising (being functionally superior to his personae in the first place) or sentimental. But the profits paid out by the Magic Thing in this area show the imposed restricted nature of the behaviour from which they are derived: bathos, nostalgia, a kind of "baffled poignancy" – or laughter at the expense of the described.

*　　　　　　　　　*　　　　　　　　　*

John Robertson: from "The Toom Meal Pock" (i.e. the Empty
Meal Bag). A popular song in Paisley around 1800, whose
message foreshadowed the Jarrow March.

> Speak no ae word about reform
> 　　Nor petition Parliament,
> A wiser scheme I'll now propose,
> 　　I'm sure ye'll gie consent –
> Send up a chiel or twa like me,
> 　　As sample o' the flock,
> Whase hollow cheeks will be sure proof
> 　　O' a hinging toom meal pock.
> 　　　　　　　　And sing, O wae's me!
>
> And should a sicht sae ghastly like,
> 　　Wi' rags, and banes, and skin,
> Hae nae impression on yon folk,
> 　　But tell ye'll stand ahin!
> O what a contrast will ye shaw
> 　　To glowring Lunnon folk,
> When in St James's ye tak' your stand,
> 　　Wi' a hinging toom meal pock.
> 　　　　　　　　And sing, O wae's me!
>
> Then rear your hand, and glow'r, and stare,
> 　　Before yon hills of beef,
> Tell them ye are frae Scotland come,
> 　　For Scotia's relief;
> Tell them ye are the verra best,
> 　　Wal'd frae the fattest flock,
> Then raise your arms, and oh! display
> 　　A hinging toom meal pock.
> 　　　　　　　　And sing, O wae's me!
>
> Tell them ye're wearied o' the chain
> 　　That hauds the state thegither,
> For Scotland wishes just to tak'
> 　　Gude nicht we ane anither.
> We canna thole, we canna bide,

This hard unwieldy yoke,
For wark and want but ill agree,
Wi a hinging toom meal pock.
And sing, O wae's me!

*   *   *

The most obvious area where the writer is usually patronising is in the depiction of speech, where for instance a writer-narrator presents standard English, and a quoted character-persona presents something else. Those apostrophes that indicate the 'and of the writer 'elping out the reader, indicating by sign the prescriptive norm from which a "character" is "deviating". The character can't talk proper words, so the writer-narrator indicates where there's bits missed out, so you can better understand. The apostrophes indicate a supposed deficiency which the reader, over the head of the persona as it were, must supply. The personae are trapped within the closed value-system that denigrates their use of language, while the writer-narrator communicates with the reader over their heads. For similar reasons any attempt to indicate specific speech sounds by secondary spelling codes, must avoid layers of puns etc. that provide nudges and winks at the speaker's expense: only by giving the speaker a consciousness that might include knowledge of these codes (i.e. so the speaker may be at least partly the author) can this be valid. In this way the speaker can implicitly refer to the nature of the codes being used and the language to which it refers.

This again though is to side with the Patient against the Doctor, to accord the little bit of present-time consciousness that can *have* a behaviour pattern rather than just *be* one. It's that area of present-time consciousness that writers like Beckett and W. S. Graham give to their personae; and the personae in turn pass it on to the reader. It's a very political thing to do, since it seems to assume that the only – and equal – value that can be placed on any human being is in the fact that the human being actually exists. Insisting on the basic equality of consciousness means rejecting the closed-value system, handing in the currency of valid being to all and sundry (increasing the money supply) and refusing to self-objectify individually or collectively.

*　　　　　　　　*　　　　　　　　*

William Finlayson: "On Three Children
in the Eastwood Churchyard" (1814)

Here lie the mouldering remains
O' three unkirsent, guiltless weans;
Wha never underwent that rite
Maks sinners mystically white;
Will ony zealot e'er presume
These early dwellers in the tomb
Wad nae admission gain in Heaven
Or that their sins were unforgiven?
Let him wi' care his Bible read,
An' to this precious text gie heed,
"Wha wad the bliss o' Heaven attain
Maun enter like a little wean."

*　　　　　　　　*　　　　　　　　*

It's in the reification of linguistic codes and their possession by dominant and powerful classes wherein lies real danger, now literally for the whole world. That reification will always contain as part of its mechanics the device to maintain the illusion that social conflict does not exist, or that such conflict as exists can be meaningfully recreated, and resolved, within its own perimeter. Self-expression outside that code becomes simply a mechanism of self-elimination. The dominant refuse to recognise that all language is an instrument of consciousness: instead, it is held as a symptom. Others don't "have" a language – they "are" it. In dismissing the language, one dismisses the existence of its users – or rather, one chooses to believe that they have dismissed themselves. The "local" becomes that which can be bombed from 30,000 feet. After all, it had chosen to cede its existence even before it was destroyed.

This happens to the past as well as to the present, and it's happened to the West of Scotland as to everywhere else. The poems inserted into this article are from a projected anthology, *Radical Renfrew*. Much of the poetry I've selected for that is committed, anti-clerical, republican; descriptive of work and poverty, with no separation between writer and persona, no "distancing" of emotion; much of it is about drink, people who enjoyed getting drunk and people who saw the suffering it caused and wrote bitterly of it, with or without satire, and with no Salvation Army tambourines jingling at the end. There's Alexander Wilson, who emigrated to America and became a pioneer American ornithologist: before he left Scotland he had been jailed for his poem "The Shark" attacking a local mill-owner, and forced to publicly burn his poem at Paisley Cross; there's his poem "The Insulted Pedlar" satirising the arrogance of a local landowner trying to drive the poet off his land with a gun when the poet was doing a shite in the landowner's field. None of the stuff is cosy. It's got nothing to do with those execrable sentimental nights out with bathos-laden songs about the slums I left behind me. It's as likely to upset the same type of people today as it would have upset a hundred years ago. And by that I don't mean it's all anti-establishment. There's James Maxwell, "Poet in Paisley" as he titled himself in the pamphlets he sold in the streets, thundering on in rhyming-couplets about how blasphemous poets might think they're smart now (1793) but they won't think that on their way to Hell. He was healthy. His mind was in his language, and he was entitled to his point of view. There's Robert Pollok of Eaglesham, whose huge "The Course of Time" – a kind of Scottish Presbyterian "Paradise Lost" – was, according to Eyre-Todd in *The Glasgow Poets*, to be found in most Scottish cottages and farmhouses throughout the nine-teenth century. My own copy is described on the title-page as "Seventy-Eighth Thousand". There's poetry as a learning device: "An Excursion Through The Starry Heavens" – a rhyming guide to the main constellations by the Reverend Robert Boog, a minister at Paisley Abbey for forty-nine years. There's poems reflecting deep personal depression, feelings of being gossiped about, the kind of work that those vanguardists with patronising attitudes to working-class people would think best forgotten as not showing "them" in a positive enough light. The political poetry – obviously including Marion Bernstein's – remains a valid interpretation of current affairs.

But these poems are not held worthy of serious consideration. They name names, articulate opinions, would carry the conflict into the living-room. And for this they have been hospitalised in the oblivion such deviance deserves. But there's another view, and it's the view that I want to put across here. Such "patients" are alive and well, and they have a multitude of things to say about the Present as well as the Past. Locality by locality, A to Z of behind-the-counter library stock, old newspaper by old newspaper, people must go on with the work of release.

Literature, Dialogue, Democracy

[Introduction to *Radical Renfrew*]

Any society is a society in conflict, and any anthology of a society's poetry that does not reflect this, is a lie. But poetry has been so defined in the public mind as usually to exclude the possibility of social conflicts appearing. The belief is widespread that poetry is not about the expression of opinion, not about "politics", not about employment, not about what people actually do with their time between waking up and falling asleep each day; not about what they eat, not about how much the food costs. It is not in the voice of ordinary discourse, contains nothing anyone anywhere could find offensive, above all contains nothing that will interfere with the lawful exercise of an English teacher going about his or her duty in a classroom.

To an extent the connection between poetry and school has been the problem. It is not that teachers deserve any less respect than anyone else out working for a living; the trouble lies in the notion that poetry has to be "taught" in the first place, and that there is a professional caste of people best equipped so to do. For to be "taught" poetry has meant to be given guidance in a classroom as to how best ultimately to pass exams about it. This has had the effect of installing in people's minds certain basic ideas:

1. A "real" poem is one that an English teacher would approve for use in an English class.
2. A "real" poem requires some explanation and guidance as to interpretation, by an English teacher.

47

3. The best poems come to be set in the exams.
4. The people best able to pass these exams will be the people best able to understand and to write poetry.

The roots of all this pernicious nonsense about what a poem isn't and what it is, can be traced back to the nineteenth-century invention of Literature as a "subject" in schools. This invention was based on certain specific principles:

1. The creation of a "canon" of Literature, the new subject's "set books" as it were.
2. The establishment of that canon – to be overseen by Her Majesty's Inspectorate for Schools – on the premise that Literature is a *code* embodying desirable social, moral and political values.
3. The exclusion from that canon of works that did not recognise this code, or did not see Literature as a code in the first place.
4. The exclusion from that canon of works whose main focus was thought properly to be that of another "subject" in the curriculum.

The important word is code. To understand Literature is to understand a code, and the teacher is the person trained to possess the code that Literature is in. This has to be accepted unconditionally, as it is the sole basis of the teacher's power to grade pupils' responses. A piece of writing that does not acknowledge the code that the teacher has been trained to possess, can not be accepted as Literature; for such writing deprives the teacher of the only basis of his power of assessment. This applies even when the "canon" has been enlarged to "allow" some writing about, for instance, working-class lives. The teacher's right to grade the pupils' responses must never be threatened; therefore the writing must never be such as might give the pupils the right to challenge the teacher's claim to possess it.

Literature shrinks to Teachable Literature. Taking a fairly

mild and non-poetic example, the excellent prose work Winwood Reade's *The Martyrdom of Man* is considered far too "literary" to be History, and far too historical to be Literature; even more damaging, it is thought far too heretical of orthodox beliefs to be thought an appropriate object for pupils' potential approval. And so it can not, as the phrase goes, "enter the canon".

In fact the spread of education as a right to the mass of people has paradoxically led to the deprivation, from them, of much they once held to be valid literature. Generation after generation has been "taught" that a poem itself has, as it were, to pass an exam before it can earn the right to be called a poem in the first place; but only those people who have passed exams about poems, can give a new would-be poem the new exam necessary to decide whether it is a poem or not. The "subject" has functioned to assure the mass of people that until they have a licence to prove otherwise, they have no public right to make, criticise, or even claim to understand, anything that might seriously be called Literature. This is a serious matter, and raises the question of what is meant by democracy.

*

In the years consequent on 1792 the most influential book circulating in Scotland besides the Bible and Burns's poems, was Tom Paine's *The Rights of Man*. This book's message was welcomed by the Paisley poet Alexander Wilson, who was soon, in 1794, to be forced into exile like Paine himself:

> "The Rights of Man" is now weel kenned,
>   And read by mony a hunder;
> For Tammy Paine the buik has penned,
>   And lent the courts a lounder;
> It's like a keeking-glass to see
>   The craft of kirk and statesman;
> And wi' a bauld and easy glee,
>   Guid faith the birky beats them
>   Aff hand this day . . .

> The power of clergy, wylie tykes,
>   Is unco fast declining;
> And courtiers' craft, like snaw aff dykes,
>   Melts when the sun is shining;
> Auld monarchy, wi' cruel paw,
>   Her dying pains is gnawing;
> While Democracy, trig and braw,
>   Is through a' Europe crawing
>   Fu' crouse this day.

The Rights of Man, which includes practical plans for family allowance, retirement and sickness pensions, and public works for the unemployed, was a sustained argument for republican democracy centred on three principles:

1. Men are born, and always continue, free and equal in respect of their rights. Civil distinctions, therefore, can only be founded on public utility.
2. The end of all political associations is the preservation of the natural and imprescriptible rights of man; and these rights are liberty, property, security, and resistance of oppression.
3. The nation is essentially the source of all sovereignty; nor can ANY INDIVIDUAL, or ANY BODY OF MEN, be entitled to any authority which is not expressly derived from it.

Paine argued that the "simple" democracy of ancient Athens was best replaced by the representational democracy of contemporary America:

> The one was the wonder of the ancient world; the other is becoming the admiration and model of the present.

This "simple" democracy of ancient Athens was simple in that all free citizens had the right, in common public assembly, to vote directly on the issues of government, face to face with those who carried them out. Moreover free citizens had the right themselves to participate in government irrespective of personal wealth. Crucial to all this was the *agora*, a central area in Athens where citizens met daily and amongst other things discussed their own business and that of the state. In the sixth century B.C. this *agora* doubled as the assembly forum where at least forty times a year issues of governance were put to the mass vote. Later the voting assembly moved ten minutes away, but its function remained the same.

Of course it was not so simple, nor so ideal. Only about a seventh of the population were "free citizens" to begin with: women, immigrants and their offspring, and slaves, were not. Yet this albeit restricted democracy had features not only unique in its own day, but in advance of those advocated for democracy in nineteenth-century Britain. And it contained two ideal principles which have not lost their force in two-and-a-half thousand years: *democracy is daily dialogue*, and *true democracy lies in the equality and equal power of all parties to that dialogue.*

The enemy of democracy, Paine argued, was the mystification of government. He argued this because mystification is the device that renders equality of dialogue impossible. With mystification, one might add, comes the caste that can be called the Keepers of the Mystery. And the Keepers of the Mystery are the Keepers of the Right to Dialogue, amongst themselves.

The invention of Literature as a teachable "subject" was the invention of Literature as a mystery – thus countering the democratic potential of the sudden expansion of literacy brought about by compulsory education. In fact the spread of the right to vote in Britain paralleled the spread of the right to literacy, in that both were allowed within formal codes whose names acknowledged the supremacy of the *status quo* which must not be challenged: Her Majesty's Government, Her Majesty's Inspectorate for Schools, the Queen's English. The rights and values of monarch and aristocracy were sown into the definitions of what the people's new entitlements to personal expression actually were. These rights and values were precisely those not acknowledged in the America where Paine and Wilson were exiled. But the Queen's English had special difficulties to

51

face in the Scotland that Wilson had left behind.

There was, in early-nineteenth-century Renfrewshire, a large number of Scots words mixed in with the English vocabulary, as the poems of Alexander Wilson and others show. But by the end of the century those words had been greatly reduced in number, and poetry written in Scots was severely restricted in content. If one looks at the annual volumes of *Modern Scottish Poetry* published between 1878 and 1893, one gets the impression of Scots poetry as being largely a male nostalgic hymn to earth, established religion, domestic gems of women, and fellow wee-boys-at-heart men. Contrary to the usual reasons given for this, this restriction in content was less to do with the diminution in vocabulary than with restrictions on content akin to those imposed on Queen's English. On the one hand Scots words and usages of any kind were barred from the diction of the classroom by teachers in their capacity as representatives of the diction of governance. On the other, changes in the language were seen as the result of an immigration substantially Irish Catholic as well as Highland Gaelic. There was a certain amount of looking back on what was seen as the once-dominant language of a single-religion people. This ignored certain realities, such as the fact that the written language used at the turn of the century by poets like Tannahill and Wilson in their informal letters to friends and equals, was almost exclusively English. More important, it concealed the fact that the poetry nostalgically looked back to was one stripped of anything that might challenge the contemporary *status quo*. *Modern Scottish Poetry*, like most late-Victorian anthologies of Scots poetry, assumes a male audience not only favourable to, but members of, the established church. That tradition of Scots poetry hostile to the *status quo* and to clergymen of any denomination; that Protestant tradition of Scots poetry expressing conflict and difference of opinion within the church itself – all this was dropped in favour of a shy alliance of writers "allowed" to keep their language going within the establishment as it was allowed to exist in Scotland. The angry became the pawky. It was anger at the end of a string.

Those most active in promoting this Scots were often those most opposed to what was actually happening in areas like Glasgow and Paisley. It was not a simple matter of locality and national culture. For with the Industrial Revolution had come the emergence in Britain of the proletarian urban dictions, and diction had become in Renfrewshire, as elsewhere in Britain, what it has never ceased to be since: not simply a matter of locality, but of class. The proletariat of the West of Scotland, Protestant or Catholic – freethinking or of any other religion, of immigrant stock or not – all could be seen as forming linguistically a colony within a colony. The new middle-class of the towns and city – who identified most with Queen's English in their diction – were often those most insistent on "good Scots" in their literary hobbies. The contempt that was heaped on the speakers of the new urban diction of the West of Scotland was based on class, and sometimes religious, prejudice as much as a desire for a return to the mythical "pure" diction of a pure race of pre-proletarian Scottish folk.

This carried into the twentieth century, as some of it has carried to this day. In an essay on John Davidson published in 1933, T. D. Robb, teacher at Paisley Grammar, and author of *Deletiae Poetarum Scotorum*, had this to say:

Davidson, as you know, adhered to English all his life, though a Renfrewshire man for over thirty years. And well he might! For what has the Doric of the populous centres of the county become? It is not Scots at all, but a thing debased beyond tears. It is a mongrel patois due to lower class immigration from Ireland, from Lancashire mills, and the meaner streets of Glasgow. Traditional vernacular is gone. The streets are sibilant with "huz yins", "wis youse", "wees wis"; ungrammatical with "I seen", "I done". Bernard Shaw's immortal line of blank verse (put into the mouth of a prize fighter),

        he seen me comin' and he done a bunk

if heard in passing through the streets, would hardly raise the eyelid of surprise. For God's sake, – to speak it with reverence – let such horrors cease to be printed as Doric. . . . Regret it as we may, the Doric of Renfrewshire is not only dead, but in an advanced state of putrefaction. "An ounce of civet, good apothecary!"

So when one hears working-class speech, whether from Scotland, Ireland or England, one should call for civet – i.e. perfume. One should call for civet, because in doing so one would be quoting from *King Lear*, Act Four, Scene Six – and if you knew that, dear reader, you were as cultured a man as T. D. Robb. One was familiar with the "canon" of English Literature.

But Robb was no eccentric then, as he would be no eccentric now. The *Scottish National Dictionary*, in its introduction of 1936, echoed his view:

> Owing to the influx of Irish and foreign immigrants in the industrial area near Glasgow the dialect has become hopelessly corrupt.

Not simply changed, but corrupted, debased. Having lost its original value. A people, in other words, for whose words issuing from their own lips one should have no respect. They had lost the right to equality of dialogue with those in possession of Queen's English, or "good" Scots. But in fact the urban dictions had, and have, connections not simply local, but world-wide. To see this one has to return to America, and Tom Paine.

*

It is no accident that the American democracy Paine so admired was made up of a mix of immigrants and their early descendants. With a new people came a new diction, and a new diction could serve as the means for an equality of dialogue. It made for an ease of conversation, one that allowed Wilson, when settled in America, informally to call not only on the similarly exiled author of *The Rights of Man* but on President

Jefferson himself. American society today is hardly a model of equality of wealth; but the openness of its Public Information Act, which contrasts so starkly with the obsessive Official Secrets Act in Britain, stems from the equality of dialogue on which the republic was founded. Similar contrasts can be made here between Britain on the one hand and Canada, Australia, and New Zealand on the other.

But the democracy of America, like those elsewhere, had been created at the expense of a native population. And just as in Ancient Athens, this democracy itself existed on the back of slave labour. There is an economic link, too, between those nineteenth-century American – and Caribbean and African – slaves, and the British urban proletariat: one group laboured long hours to extract raw materials which the other laboured long hours to finish into manufactured goods. This historic link survived in the language of the groups, and in the Literature of the children and grandchildren of those slaves and proletariat writing today. In Scotland the links are the more close because of the colony-within-a-colony aspect already mentioned. The language presents writers with a similar range of options, and prompts similar highly political questions: whether the use of English modelled on middle-class English writers is an acceptance of colonial status; whether the use of words from the pre-colonial era is justified when the pre-colonial vocabulary is now obsolete or greatly reduced; whether a model of the language as spoken, with mainly Anglified vocabulary but non-English syntax and/or sound, is restricted to being the model of an individual speaker speaking. Always the criticism of "provincialism": but it's an international pattern, and not just in the former English Empire. It is simply the right to equality of dialogue that is being fought for. Yet when one sees the historic connection between slave and proletariat embodied in the language, one sees more clearly the actual nature of derisive laughter at working-class speech and accent today; one sees what forces are behind the vehemence with which a child will be told to alter his or her language when addressing a superior; one sees too clearly the connection between "light-hearted" guides to "slang" and the lovable cheery black servants of pre-war American films.

But it isn't just the right to equality of dialogue in the present that has to be established, but equality of dialogue with the past. A person must feel free to go back into the past that is Literature, go where they like and meet equally with whom they will. If a model of Literature has been created that prevents this, that model should be removed, and with it the metaphors that restrict the open nature of people's access. There has been enough of Literature as a "path" through the ages, as a "course" entrusted to those appointed to "its" charge. Let a writer have the authority to address any reader – and any reader to read any writer – without either feeling that valid dialogue can only take place in a code acceptable to a transmitter of the code of governance – in other words, within the code of governance itself. Let a writer have the authority to be nobody else but themself, if they so wish: to make direct reference to specific particulars of their own life, as lived, names and all. But the code of governance of the "canon" specifically *excludes* any person from being "nobody else but themself". This is the heart of the mystery: it is the "unwritten constitution" of what is "taught" as British Literature. Unwritten indeed.

The ludicrous nature of McGonagall's work, for instance. McGonagall's naïvety was not in being nobody else but himself. It was in being nobody else but himself in a code that did not allow him to be nobody else but himself in the first place. But why should a code of governance exclude anyone from being nobody else but themselves? What could be the point of this? The answer, it seems to me, is that a code of Literature could not be thought desirable in which anyone might imagine that, by being nobody else but themselves, they were the equal of anyone else. It would be not be thought desirable, that is, to a government expressly founded on the principle that not everyone is equal to anyone else at all, but there is a "natural" inequality which people have to be taught. One has to recognise that the concession of parliamentary democracy in Britain was not the concession that all human beings are equal. At this point I am driven to try to define what I mean by all human beings being equal. Of course to try will be an act of gross impertinence on my part, as I am a human unlicensed to define such things as what a human is. However, I will try to do so in two paragraphs, in as simple a language as I can. This isn't easy, but it is worth a try.

I would not describe myself as "the" human being; that would mean I thought that no other human being existed, or that others weren't quite as much a human being as I am. I understand fully that I am just "a" human being, just as anyone else is just "a" human being as well. But of course like you the reader, whoever you are, I am *not* just anyone else – I am "this" human being that nobody else is.

The stages can be seen like the stages between being a baby – when the universe is no more than the baby itself – and being an adult. Growing up is learning to accept that you are just "a" human being, that others are like yourself equal in that they are human and that they exist as well. The trouble starts when people are taught they can go from being "the" human being when they open their eyes on the world, to being "this" human being in adulthood, without having to swallow that they are just "a" human being in between. Then they think that whatever it is makes them "this" human being is what stops them being just "a" human being in the first place.

This, in my opinion, is the model of the basis of British government that has produced a specifically British model of education that has produced a specifically British model of Literature. To go simply to the model of education: a tawdry chain of privilege runs downwards from the likes of Eton and Winchester, down to the expensive private schools of Scotland and elsewhere, down finally to the less expensive schools of town and city, whose pupils, though they may not be the equal of those from Eton and Winchester, can at least know they are distinctly superior to the scruff in the free school down the road. Inequality of status of diction has been one peculiarly British way of sorting people into a hierarchy of worth. But enough of that too, it has been but one way amongst others. Sufficient to say, and to say it with double force in Scotland, that no language is more sacred than the people who speak it; more to the point, no language is more sacred than the people who don't.

A Literature in which it is possible for a writer to be nobody else but his or her own self, would not be "an enormous extension to the present model of Literature" or some such; it can only happen within a new model of Literature altogether, one that rejects inequality as a constituent of personal being to begin with. So it isn't the addition of "community" to "high" culture. That assumes their separation; that is the product of the old model of "subject", of "path", of ownership of certain values by certain people. But if you are free to go where you like as an equal in Literature, then you don't "cross into zones" and put on a "serious literature" or "local literature" hat. You don't have to give any explanations to anybody as to why you're there; nor does the writer have to give any explanation to you. It's all one Literature, as it is all one world.

This is what makes the use of *King Lear*, for instance, as a way of putting people "in their place", so awful: *King Lear* is, among other things, about a monarch's coming to terms with the fact that he's a human being the equal, no more, of all others; having to face the reality of his place in a world where dogs, horses and rats can have life when his own daughter can't. This recognition of the equality of human beings is part of what makes it impossible to be the "property" of any particular person or class. James Thomson's poem "The City of Dreadful Night" also takes this equality as given, which is why it connects as easily with "community" as with "high" art.

The poem, by some Community versus High Art ways of looking at things, might be thought ripe for the "elitist" tag. It has subtitle quotes from Dante and Leopardi, and links with other European writers such as Novalis; it can even be seen, in terms of its underlying shape and tone – its long circular movements of thought, its building up of counterpointed blocks of logic, its brooding seriousness throughout; its pauses, its final climaxes presenting images that summarise the preceding themes – as being organised like a "typical" symphony of Thomson's contemporary, the Austrian composer Anton Bruckner.

But even my discussing this might be thought "elitist" to some and a bit uppity to others. To the latter in one way I am "breaking the code" of Literary Criticism by moving from Literature into Music, but as it's Classical Music I've moved into, that's probably all right so long as I seem to be verifying the "authority" of both. But it would not be all right for me to say that it doesn't actually matter a damn whether you the reader actually like Bruckner or not; it doesn't matter whether you've even heard of him. To say so would be me being nobody else but myself, telling you that you have the right to be nobody else but yourself as well: this, at the expense of the authority of "the canon" of classical music. But whether or not Bruckner ever wrote a note of music doesn't matter in the sense that it has nothing to do with the value of you – or me – as human beings. Neither Music nor Literature, nor any other art, *puts* value into people. Yet it's because of this very fact as a given (although we have been taught to assume the opposite) that I claim the freedom to mention Bruckner if I want to, without being called "elitist": I happen to like his music a lot, that liking has led me to see a connection with Thomson that might interest you, and my liking for Bruckner is part of "this" human being that is me and nobody else. Which is an aspect of the way that James Thomson proceeds in "The City of Dreadful Night" . . .

Once you accept that the model of Literature is based on universal equality of human existence, past and present, then you can travel in Literature, as a writer or as a reader, wherever you like. And it is not a "broad-based subject" – "Open Literature" or "Social Studies" – with a new caste charged to grade the responses of those who approach "it", that I'm talking about; for it is that very system of grading and exams which turns the living dialogue between writer and reader into a thing, a commodity to be offered in return for a bill of exchange, i.e. the certificate or "mark". But no caste has the right to possess, or even to imagine it has the right to possess, bills of exchange on the dialogue between one human being and another. And such a dialogue is all that Literature is.

*

The place where a democratic freedom of encounter with Literature has occurred is in the free public libraries. It is not that they haven't operated censorship, but the public libraries have remained the one place where anyone can build his or her own relation with the literary world. It was in the public library in Pollok that I built mine. The five-to-seven department, just a green tin cupboard with about eight shelves, and the books facing out the way. You had to wrap your books in newspaper, and you had to show your hands. Then the day when I could use the Junior Department for the 7–14s: a whole wall under the windows. Real books at last, that wouldn't be finished as soon as you got home. Of course the time came when the Junior Department wasn't what I wanted, but I wasn't old enough yet for the adult. I got to know the names of the authors in the A to C section of the adult section that adjoined the Junior wall at the far end. The adult fiction went right round two walls of the building, with non-fiction in standing shelves between. What a day that would be, when you could get into that. My mother let me take the bus to Govan to use the Junior Department at Elder Park. It seemed enormous, as big as Pollok's adult section; it had a very quiet atmosphere I'll never forget, with really heavy stone walls, and the pillars you went in at the entrance. It was there I got to know Dickens. Then the adult section at Pollok. Then the Stirling, the Mecca of them all.

The public libraries gave me the education I wanted. Like most Scottish writers I know of my generation, I went to school and got British – mainly English – Literature, I went to the library and borrowed American, Russian and European. And these were the ones that mattered as far as I was concerned. When the hero of *Crime and Punishment* ran down the stairs of a close after the murder, I knew what it was he ran down. All the poetry that meant anything to me in my middle teens, when I first got to like poetry – all of it that meant anything to me, I got out the library. You could choose what you wanted there, read it in your own house, say exactly what you wanted about it, or – most precious right of all – you could say absolutely nothing about it whatever.

In my early twenties I worked in a university bookshop. I hated it. You might as well have been selling bananas, and the pay was rubbish. A non-union place, I was young, and it took the work inspectorate to call and pin up the minimum work-shop rates for me to find out I was being paid less than the legal minimum for shopworkers. I decided to try to get to University, and studied at night to make up my Highers. At dinner time I would sometimes make it to the library at St George's Cross, and get a quick half hour in in the reading room. Other times in the Mitchell Library at Charing Cross, not getting on with my Highers but sitting with a book called *The Annotated Index to the Cantos of Ezra Pound*, writing in tiny pencil in the margin of my own copy of Pound's poems, the references from the index. This was my education.

I did get in to University, and at the second attempt got the degree in English and Scottish Literature that gave me the bit of paper that now matters to me. That paper I renew every year for £5; the membership card to Glasgow University Library. That Library is specialised, and offers a special-ised view of the world. Its filters have excluded literature by working-class people, though there are books in plenty about "them". You have to go elsewhere for original literature itself.

In some ways it's here that the public libraries come into their own, and in others it's where they have been most frustrating. The public libraries have been where millions including myself have received that education beyond basic literacy that actually mattered to them; but while the public has been out-front borrowing the books, through the back there has always been that world you see over the librarian's shoulder when they go to phone, those rooms with half-open doors marked "Private" that they put the light on in when they go through. Always when I have requested a book at the issue desk of the Mitchell Reference Library in Glasgow, and when someone has later appeared to hand the book over at the counter, there has been that pleasant smile between us as if Isn't it lucky a wee fairy turned up with the right book just out of sight round the corner. And always I've thought at the back of my mind, I wonder what it looks like where you've been.

It was therefore a great thing to me when I was given the job as "Writer in Residence" at Paisley Central Library. Besides running writers' groups and meeting people who wanted a response to their writing, I was given the freedom to go wherever I wanted behind the counter, and unlike the staff who are always busy having to be librarians, I could stop wherever I wanted and read whatever I liked. Paisley, besides being a public lending library, holds the main large collection of non-borrowable books in Renfrew District Libraries: books that are too rare or flimsy to be going in and out on public loan. They are all available for the public to read though in the reference section – but like any other reference library, you can't really get to know the collection from a cabinet index. You don't feel like asking the librarian to fetch you up twenty books to see what ones you like. It's only by physically having them in your hand you can get to know the range of them. That privilege was given to me in my job, and this anthology from the local poetry collection in the reference-room gallery is the result.

The Present Tense

a semi-epistolary romance

Ah, Sun-flower! weary of time

(William Blake)

Lyk as the dum
Solsequium
With cair ou'rcum

(Alexander Montgomerie)

. . . The ocean, grinding stones,
Can only speak the present tense

(Robert Lowell)

This one a fiction. That we knew nothing, ***************
***.
The kind that ******************************** because
we're masochists at heart. That doesn't want to be thought too
systematically intelligent, ******************************
** To be lovable
****************************** then to complain about
it, all the time, all the time.

Time – time, time, time, time, time. Better to be drunk and
randomly   intelligent,   *******************************
for which you cannot be held responsible, *************
***************** and for which you can be held responsible, because you are saying it. So you can be responsible for
your intelligence but innocent of it. *******************
****************************** will make you lovable,
that in your own innocence ***********************.

The model. The model is a model of literature is a model of
language is a model of consciousness, that includes reader and
writer as existing at the same time. That paradox, that conceit.
That's what the fucking model is.

*

*Anyway. It's the nature of the Present Tense, that's what I've
been worrying at this past how long, in sickness and in health.
I made this analysis on dBASE 11 of 100 poems by fifty poets,
two each, chosen more or less at random from my shelves. I
made several lists, poet, poem, tense, reference, attitude, form*

and so on. Kept thinking of new categories not so much to categorise them as to force myself to articulate my feelings, and to compare poems, especially different schools that usually have a brick wall separating them. It took me long enough to notice that fully 95 out of the 100 contained the Present Tense in some form or another. I say in some form or another because of course it wasn't the same Present Tense that was being used at all, no sirree, yet the type of Present Tense used tended to be the fundament on which the structure was built.

It was the fundament in that it was that which carried the crunch, one way or another. It was that which let you know where the writer was speaking from, what was the place of address, whether there was room in it for you – and whether the described person, the subject of the poem or whatever, was actually existing in that world or was already stuffed and on the wall for the writer to write the name-tag and fill in the habitat.

*

. . . I resolved to take a terrible revenge. A hatchet was fetched . . . whether the shock to the whole framework of the secretary was responsible, I do not know, but I do know that a secret drawer sprang open, one which I had never before noticed. This opened a pigeonhole that I naturally had never discovered. Here to my great surprise I found a mass of papers, the papers which form the content of the present work. (Kierkegaard, *Either/Or*)

I think there's something wrong with my liver. (Dostoevsky, *Notes from Underground*)

I must apologise for having persuaded my patient to write his autobiography . . . I take my revenge by publishing them, and I hope he will be duly annoyed. (Svevo, *Confessions of Zeno*)

I offer no remarks on it, and make as few additions to it, leaving every one to judge for himself. (Hogg, *Confessions of a Justified Sinner*)

These notebooks were found among Antoine Roquentin's papers. We are publishing them without alteration. (Sartre, *Nausea*)

And it is only the wish to be useful that has prompted me to publish these fragments of a diary that came into my hands accidentally. (Lermontov, *A Hero of Our Time*)

Attacked in early youth by an abominable moral malady, I here narrate what happened to me during the space of three years. (De Musset, *The Confessions of a Child of the Century*)

I climb onto my bed . . . Some crumbling cornicing, two loose bricks, some loose plaster; an opening is revealed to my eyes, big as my hand, but invisible from below, due to the cornice-work. I look . . . I gaze . . . the room next door presents itself to me, completely exposed. (Barbusse, *Hell*)

*

Anyway. It takes you to a discussion of literature as a model of diction versus literature as a model of meaning, or lexical intensity; punctuation as a signpost to breath or as organiser of areas of semantic yield. This side of the Atlantic, Finnegans Wake's *the big crossroads followed by Beckett's stuff circa 1945–52. Or maybe not, Mr Wayside Pulpit.*

I'd like to link the whole bloody lot up. Not just literature, I mean THE LOT. Sometimes your brain just about seizes up you get that feeling, that tremendous feeling of the pattern, like a great big mesh where suddenly everything lights up because you see the same electricity suddenly coursing through all these different things. It's gone in a flash of course though during that flash it's as if you get this deep breath of air that you know is there all the time, but usually you can't get at it.

Breath, breath, breath, breath, breath. If only Winnicott had gone further with that aside about the baby's first perception of breath, median between inner and outer, its role as the point at which the defences are down. Maybe he did, I just haven't seen it. So much of his stuff is great, so exciting to read. All that stuff about the sucking-blankets (his "guggie", mine used to call it) "transitional objects" and their relation to culture, the first experience of symbols in time. That "potential space" where play occurs . . . "It is play that is the universal, and that belongs to health." Good on you, Mr Winnicott. A very healthy man.

*

30 WEDNESDAY Ironic that those most concerned to emphasise the importance of what is now called "orature" are often the people most hostile to any indication of oral pronunciation. There is literature, and there is the oral. The oral written down is orature. But there must be no vestige of the fact of orality emphasised in the transcription. This would be as it were to move to the viscous, the existential, away from Word as that thing in itself which is pronounced. Word is a serious thing, its serious thingness should not be threatened by the interpolation of that which would leave the vestige of utterance as part of its description. To indicate the act of the individual speaker in the utterance is to "debase" the word and to question the common reality of that to which it refers.

There is a congruence here with certain conservative folklorists who like to see themselves as defenders of the true People's Culture against all these experimentalists, elitist wankers, etc. The fact is that "orature" is taken as having an inbuilt duty to be revered, though you always know you're in the presence of Death when reverence and art are bound together. It's reverence for the Word supposedly common to orature and literature that arouses hostility and a defensive contempt when a viscous link between the two is presented. One reason is that indication of pronunciation drags the present into that past from which the Word is supposed unobtrusively to have been launched. It is vital to protect the pastness of that past, because in so doing one can present the fixity and inevitability of tradition. The function therefore of the artist is to act "responsibly" towards that fixed tradition, and a fixed tradition is insecure without the fixity of Word. Hence to challenge that fixity of word by site-specifying it in the mouth of a particular speaker, is to behave "irresponsibly".

*

Trouble with these people who identify the unconscious with a linguistic structure I think is that it can so easily drift into this authority-based thing. It's that perennial tendency you always have to be on your guard against, those who want to construct a "natural law" that's prescriptive. Or as somebody I read once put it, whenever moralists have recourse to biology you know there's a reactionary viewpoint coming up.

Have you read Eriugena, the Irish 9th century geezer? Not that I've learnt him off by heart myself, but he's got some prrretty interesting things to say about words, thought, all that sort of trade. He thinks our very own Blessed Trinity, which is to say Evans Stein and Peacock (sorry, that's facetious) has a structure that corresponds to the structure of language and its relation to thought. Reminds me of some of our 20th-century bods in his own way. Not that I'd ever say anything about him in public of course you know the way it is unless you can name every stop between Auchenshuggle and Clydebank you're not supposed to get on the tram. "Ignorance of the divine nature is true wisdom; by not knowing it is best known." That's Eriugena, or John Scotus to you. Of course you'll put it down to "the rhetorical nihilism of the Celt".

*

14 TUESDAY . . . The play as ritual. What remains is to create a structure of shared existence . . . the created "characters" are condemned not to become "interesting". For something of narrative interest to happen would be to destroy the motive energy of their existence.

It's not that nothing interesting really happens. But the events of interest are always towards — or an undermining of — a definition of the people to whom they do. What I mean by that is that there are not "people" to whom things happen: the happenings are in a sense the continued inability of the separate people satisfactorily to define themselves.

There's an ambivalence in the central existence of the characters. This is both as performers of the play itself, which has become ritual, and for the presentation of their own existence at that moment, which it is tacitly understood must never be allowed to lapse into irony – like the actor who hogs the show with private jokes to the audience.

Rothenberg: "I do think that part of our yearning has been to save for ourselves the possibility of a ritualised experiencing of the world – as something sacred. So that the term you use, 'a ritual entertainment', involves a kind of paradox, or raises the question in any particular instance: is it ritual, with the serious function and meaning that rituals have, or is it, as they say, mere entertainment? I'm aware too that this is a rather complicated question, that even in traditional societies where we seem to see ritual at its most intense and religious, there is a kind of entertainment/simple pleasure in the activity that draws many of the participants into the ritual event. And ritual devoid of entertainment can be the most agonising bore and obligation."

(Riverside Interviews No. 4)

*

MacNeice	Woods	Pa+Pr	"these Woods are", we walk out we?
MacSweeney	Ode Grey Ros	Pres	"damn is dam" "revives" among rand imag
MacSweeney	Ode Stem Hai	Pres	"phantoms energise" etc imag/paint const
Magill	La Basee Rd	Pres	Marching "each day" now + pr in Fu & Past
Magill	Listng Patrl	Pres	what "I" sold hear each night + addr read
Muldoon	The Sightsee	Past	n/a
Muldoon	Cherish the	Pr+Pa	double "as it is" "in this poem he opens"
Neruda	Walking Arou	PrFsu	"I want to see no more" images of destr
Neruda	The Portrait	Pa+Pr	Mem of persecuted + in stone "he lives"
Olson	Maximus, to	Pa+Pr	rem + rep "we grow up many" here "I look

Olson	The Kingfish	Pr+Pa	multiple, hist + opinion + un & sp desc
Paulin	Descendancy	Pres	Un, opinion + cousin drives +"could be"
Paulin	Foot Patrol	Apres	mid after "they hold" rifles + morWhyisit
Raworth	Conscience o	Pres	image-reflections "in this ward" etc.
Raworth	Wandering	Upr.H	"lost and am fishing" self addr images
Redgrove	Rescue Pres	unclear	imag-seq The doctor booms
Redgrove	Florent Past	n/a	
Rosenberg	Returning We	Pr+Pa	"night is", we hear, + univ ab girls
Rosenberg	Through Thes	Pres	Jews "these cold days" "They see"
Rothenberg	Pirate, The	Pa+Pr	narr of pilgrim "who eats iron?" etc.
Rothenberg	Poland 1931–	Upres	dram mon address to poland "my mind is"
Sorescu	The Glass Wa	Pa+Pr	berlin wall allegory, in which we live
Sorescu	The Complain	Past	dram mon "here at the last judgement"
Stevens	The Public S	Pr+Pa	described archit "as when a jan bears"
Stevens	Of Modern Po	Upres	Of poetry, what "It has to be living" etc.
Thomas D	And Death Sh	Fut	n/a

*

how cum

    the how dumb deid

        ach

let me take yi back

    tay the midnineteen sixties

        the setting is glasgow

gateway to barrhead

    the birthplace of john davidson

        headbanger and poet

who is irrelevant to our tale

    the setting is glasgow

        the place a bookshop

ach

    robbe-grillet

        notes from underground

the divided self

    gide's journals

        pascal's pensees

edward glover

either/or

watt and molloy

a hero of our time

ach

these books and others

birling in the head

of the hero of our tale

lonely in a bookshop

sexually fucked up

given to hard drinking

and little ambition

not yet political

not yet in london

not yet with a baby

and a landlord

who didn't like babies

or rent books ach

About government, in relation to what you say. I have a book out the university library just now, a very exciting read, a book from which I will be taking some notes before returning it. The book is called Lobbying Government *and is by far the clearest guide to the actual wielders of power in government that I have come across. It is written, with the help of MPs and government officials, by an adviser aiming the book at corporate directors wishing to use the government, as he puts it, "as a tool". It is not a left-wing book, which makes for very interesting reading of such as the table (the book is full of clear tables) which lists on a mark-out-of-ten basis those who have actual power: the single MP is bottom of the league (1 out of 10) whilst the Commons Chamber amasses 2 out of 10: comment "Façade of democracy". The new policy of farming out government officials to private industry, before they then go back into government, of course also makes for interesting reading, as is the layer of industrial "policy advisers". Not that the book names names but if you read the business pages of the papers at all there's plenty to choose from. Jeffrey Sterling of P & O is the most visible example, policy adviser at the Department of Trade and Industry, snugly ensconced on the Cabinet privatisation committee, also advising on broadcasting — and chairman of the same P & O that went for the seamen's union like Thatcher went for the miners, only a year after the Zeebrugge disaster that cost so many lives. Are P & O to be prosecuted for poor safety standards? No — because P & O have given the Tory Party over £100,000 this past three years, was Labour's accusation. The deliberate blurring of the distinction between industrialist and government official is shown in Scotland just now — the so-called "plan for growth" operated by a group of major industrialists as official advisers to Rifkind, the usual Tory chums-gang, who needs a civil service now. There's our own bonny Michael Forsyth, author of several nutcase right-wing pamphlets about putting private tenders in to the public services, boss of a PR firm with a private cleaning services company on its list – and now snugly ensconced as minister at the departments of health and education. There's the latest "leak" from the Department of Overseas Aid, which makes it known that the government wishes, along with the Americans, to launch a scheme by which those countries requiring aid could have "help" to have their nationalised industries privatised. There's the latest news, within the past few days, of the "consortium" that is bidding to take over the General Electric Company, a huge thing worth billions, in the care of which there are a lot of Britain and America's most advanced and secret military work. The head of G.E.C. is, or was till recently, Jim Prior, former government minister. The chairman of the merchant bank putting the bid together on behalf of the consortium is John Nott – former Minister of Defence.*

One could go on, and on. The main point I'd just make is that I can't stand "Yes Minister" and I can see why it is supposed to be Thatcher's favourite programme. It puts forward the idea that ministers are essentially decent bumbling people in the grip of Red Tape civil servants who are a Drain On The Taxpayer. That officials can tie up a minister and carry their own policies from government to government, the Lobbying Government *book makes clear. But the present set of ministers are neither benign, nor bumbling. They are in fact very efficient, and very logical indeed. And the civil service is on their side.*

*

10 SUNDAY Literature as dialogue. To travel anywhere, past and present, in equality of dialogue. Area of encounter as hologram. As model of the universe. As *agora*. This time no exclusions. First slave to be freed, the reader. Three-dimensional plan, to which added the dimension of personal existence, which is inseparable from Time.

The usual straight-line metaphors of tradition's path, course, etc. Their relation to imposed concepts of deviance. Their invalidation of personal existence.

Blake's "Mock On Mock On". The kinetics of the thought of the first two verses. The argument between images of directioning and two-dimensionality. The three-dimensionality of "Israel's tents" in the last verse. The world in the grain of sand.

*

[The relationship between the formalistic rigidities of theology as the narrator experienced it and the emotional inhibitions which can ensue is nowhere more carefully indicated than in the second story of *Dubliners*, "An Encounter". The stranger in the second story is in fact a metamorphosis of Father Flynn from the first. Of the priest, "When he smiled he used to uncover his big discoloured teeth" (p. 11); of the stranger, "The man, however, only smiled. I saw that he had great gaps in his mouth between his yellow teeth" (p. 23). The stranger is dressed "in a suit of greenish black" (p. 22); the priest's clothes (black, presumably) have been discoloured by snuff, "which gave his ancient priestly garments their green faded look" (p. 10). The priest, as I have already quoted, smiles "pensively" as he puts the young boy through his paces learning the mass off by heart; he also shows the boy how "complex and mysterious were certain institutions of the Church", through his questions; the stranger, talking about girls, "gave me the impression that he was repeating something which he had learnt by heart" (p. 24) — and, going on about chastisement, "He described to me how he would whip such a boy, as if he were unfolding some elaborate mystery" (p. 25). The stranger's voice, "as he led me monotonously through the mystery, grew almost affectionate and seemed to plead with me that I should understand him" (p. 25); in his dream, the young boy sees the priest's face, and he tries to think "of Christmas", but "the grey face still followed me. It murmured; and I understood that it desired to confess something" (p. 9).

It's because of this steady accumulation of circumstantial

evidence that one is able to see the relevance of juxtaposing the reference to the priest's failure to live up to the ritual in the first story, and the stranger's private ritual when he walks away from the boys in the second:

1. "It was that chalice he broke . . . That was the beginning of it. Of course, they say it was all right, that it contained nothing, I mean. But still . . . They say it was the boy's fault." (p. 15)

2. "After a silence of a few minutes, I heard Mahony exclaim:
   'I say, Look what he's doing!'
   As I neither answered nor raised my eyes, Mahony exclaimed again:
   'I say . . . He's a queer old josser!' " (p. 24)   ]

*

FIRE   As kingfishers catch fire, dragonflies draw flame
WATER As tumbled over rim on roundy wells
EARTH Stones ring; like each tucked string tells, each hung bell's
AIR   Bow swung finds tongue to fling out broad its name;
       Each mortal thing does one thing and the same
       Deals out that being indoors each one dwells;
       Selves – goes itself; myself it speaks and spells,
       Crying, What I do is me: for that I came

Ring out wild bells: ing, ing, ing, ung, ung, ung, ing, ing, ing, ing/ ells, ells, ells, eals, ells, elves, elf, elf, ells –

Copleston: "It is not so easy to understand exactly what this *haecceitas* or *entitas singularis vel individualis* or *ultima realitas entis* actually is. It is, as we have seen, neither matter nor form nor the composite thing. A human being, for instance, is *this* composite being, composed of *this* matter and *this* form . . . it seems to be implied that a thing has *haecceitas* or 'thisness' by the fact that it exists."

*

CLASS middle y/n working y/n ex-working educated tertiary y/n REFERENCE topical/ real world/interpretation of events/politics/in the world/restricted world PREOCCUPA-TIONS domestic/ideological/academic VOICE shouted/quiet/interior/exterior/earnest/ private school/comprehensive/commitment y/n anger y/n personal y/n group implied y/n honest y/n BREATH private/public-declam/personal/narrative/dramatic/exact of diction y/n sentences y/n utterance y/n intimate/self revelatory/fake self revelatory EMOTION primary y/n humour y/n personal irony y/n despair y/n sarcastic y/n presumed shared anger y/n TONE earthy/gutsy/exasperated/tender/beautiful/self deflating/self aggrandising/self disappearing/self hiding/trying to convince you/ assuming you're not there/tone the justification for hidden premises PERSON evidently present/secondary/male-build/female-building/persona-isolating/isolates others/ subjects presumed to be not part of audience/part of group/group in audience presumed/ men y/n women y/n race y/n class y/n disdain for w/c culture y/n disdain for m/c culture y/n presumed victim/hetero y/n gay y/n whiffy y/n SEX lust/abstracted/pantheist/life-force/metaphysical/coded for audience approval/difficult to think of this writer having sex/tone that suggests passion is inferior MEANING overt/disguised/presumed/fake "objective"/difficult to understand/specific concrete/abstract nouns as subject/thing primary/detailed/provides information/moral primary/moralist/parable maker/subject as instance of a moral/ VERIFYING AUTHORITY structure y/n social group y/n person y/n culture y/n coded for integration-into-larger-model etc y/n anti-integratory y/n PLACE poetry hall/pub/church/classroom/street/where the reader is/ TOPOGRAPHY domestic/ industrial/rural/national/urban/allegory/literary/real environment/environment as parable/ VARIETY tone y/n reference y/n structure y/n rhythm y/n

*

Anyway. As the chap says, From Coppernickers to Warhole, "we have witnessed the destabilisation of the subject of the subject-centred universe and the rise of a cultural physics that places the mobility of the sign at the de-centred centre of all discourses." Which is to say, Fuck me with a broombrushed

Mars Bar. "Wot *is a wery phallocentric remark, Samivel.*"
Shall we go? (They run like fuck.)

*

PERSON CENTRED VERSUS AUTHORITY CENTRED

 Present tense meaning recurring things, given constants abstract and concrete

 Present tense meaning the present day, contemporary events, etc.

 Present you're in yourself, specific consciousness here & now

 Present the thing's in, i.e. as object

 Present inside the thing, language of personae, etc.

 Present the narrator's in

 Present the author's in, specific there & then

 Planck's constant

The dolls not solid. At least not necessarily. The choice whether each has access to the other, e.g. is a persona caged in a present inside the present of the narrator, reified in a defining action beyond whose perimeter there is no exit. The stereotype as false universal. Existence given in a supposed universal present between writer and reader – on condition that a spurious "archetype" is denied the humanity that could have similar access (e.g. might read the work themselves).

Sterne: "I leave this void space that the reader may swear into it any oath that he is accustomed to." If the time isn't closed off, it can't be the medium for an authority deemed to have had the last word.

*

"Mach's book" illusion. Retinal movement not a necessary factor: cf. prosody link between line ending and pause, *vide* Olson's ubiquitous projective verse essay. V-day also 1909 Encyc. Brit. entry on projective geometry. Bon voyage!

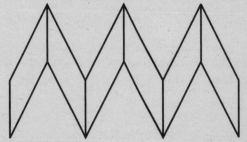

If I would have begun this sentence with a conditional pluperfect subjunctive, it is the ambiguity of "this" that allows me to conclude in the present . . . And so on.

*

When I started reading all that quantum and relativity stuff again I started getting these headaches, I thought I'd better watch it but it was ok. I think I've grasped it to an extent, not to keep up with it, I can never follow the algebra etc., but so long as I can keep within sight of the smoke from the fire over the horizon, reasonably apt image, I'll be quite happy. I had this idea about juxtaposing particle, wave, string; noun, verb, sentence; phoneme, morpheme, word. "Wire it all up to synaptic function. Plug all the bastards in to the double helix. Put it on at the Traverse. The male as particle, the female as wave. Puir wee particles. Always trying to be a straight line."

Just a thocht, though not really what it's about. I read one of them, quite refreshing after a really detailed state-of-the-art, not too compromising, ipse dixit, *"But what is now? There is no such thing in physics; it is not even clear that 'now' can ever be described, let alone explained, in terms of physics." That's the wee beastie that's always had me, the contradiction in a sentence like, "I am presently thinking." That shortfall to infinity, ten to the power minus twenty-four seconds, and still travelling. Not that it's the subatomic concept of virtual time or something that bothers me. It's the here-and-now size almost just big enough to understand, that I never understand. If you see what I mean. Anyway.*

*

Parliament. The ritualisation of the concept of dialogue. Imprimatur. Nihil obstat. Toot toot, sweetie pie.

What Happens in
Reznikoff's Poetry

Charles Reznikoff died ten years ago in New York on January 22nd, 1976. Since then Black Sparrow have issued the complete poetry: *Complete Poems 1918–75* (2 vols), *Testimony: The United States 1885–1915* (2 vols), and *Holocaust*. It seems clear to me, looking at this work, that Reznikoff is one of the very great writers of this century. Why more people don't share this opinion, I'm not sure. Maybe they haven't read him. Maybe this article might encourage them at least to give him a try.

His work manages to convey a deep sense of the existential, of the solitariness of the here-and-now (where "only the narrow present is alive") with a deep sense of history, and of his place and responsibility as a human being in history. For most writers a genuine sense of one – the existential or the historic – is purchased at the expense of the other. But in Reznikoff the imagist (of the moment of existence) and the narrative (of the timespan) co-exist; they co-exist through collocation, collocation of fragments in numbered sequences that make artistic wholes. These sequences Reznikoff usually printed and published himself, from 1918 until 1969 – when he was 73 years of age.

A good basic comparison for his technique, as for so much of American poetry from imagism through William Carlos Williams, "objectivism", Robert Creeley and Black Mountain, can be found in painting. While the poetic line was seen as the key to diction – pause the end of each line, a point still not grasped by many a True Brit – it could also be seen as the basic "plane" as in cubism, to provide as it were ways of "angling the meanings" against one another in a poem. This involved a disruption of conventional syntax; one need go no further than Williams's *Pictures from Brueghel* (starting with the title sequence) to study this. But Reznikoff does not collocate "angles of meaning" from line to line. To that extent, albeit he uses the line as a unit of rhythmic diction, he still does not disrupt traditional syntax. His collocation, juxtaposition of different senses of a whole, is from section to section within an overall sequence: these sections, be they of one line or of three hundred, are on the one hand self-sufficient, in their plain phrase or narrative, but in an important way they are all, in every sequence and without exception, fragmentary.

I think I can best explain what I mean by saying that the image I have of Reznikoff's work as a whole is like that of a great cubist hologram. The angles, or planes of this cubist hologram are made up of hundreds of sections of his major sequences. These angles or planes can be seen as representing different aspects of consciousness and behaviour: moments of consciousness of an isolated individual, walking the streets of New York; incidents and moments of consciousness of sundry urban Americans; ditto (in a manner recalling *Dubliners*) of sundry specifically Jewish individuals in an American ghetto of the past; incidents of significance to the Jewish people as a whole, from scripture to the Russian pogroms of 1905; incidents from post-war trial records of the Nazi attempt to destroy the whole Jewish race; incidents from legal records – especially with relation to crime and industrial accidents – pertaining to Americans nation-wide between 1885 and 1915. There are, in all, 1,087 verse sections making up the sequences that are Reznikoff's poetry: *Testimony* has 460 sections, *Holocaust* has 54, and the *Complete Poems 1918–75* has 573. While reading them I took brief notes to remind me of their contents: what follows is a selection from my notebooks, made whilst reading the books in the order mentioned in the last sentence. The words in italics, note, are mine, not Reznikoff's. I have interspersed quotes from the poems themselves.

Husband beats baby to death with belt because it won't stop crying when he's home for lunch.
Man kills neighbour over son going out with 16-year-old daughter.
Negro crushed to death loading boiler has funeral paid for on understanding no claim against company.
Immigrant shouted at by foreman puts hand into cotton machine where knives are just a blur.
Woman has eye put out by bunch of drunk boys annoying train passengers.
Orphan 12-year-old girl whipped and burnt by foster-mother for not doing ironing.
15-year-old told to hold 40–45lb belt for machine up ladder. Falls, arm torn off at elbow.

> The shaft was running at full speed
> as he put the ends of the belt over it
> and dropped them down
> and he was starting back when the machinist called
>   up,
> "Go back and hold that belt!"
> He did and was holding the belt up from the shaft in
>   a loop
> for about ten minutes
> when the machinist called up again,
> "Wait! I am going to get some lacing."
> The boy became tired and moved his feet a little
> the plank turned —
> and he fell on the shaft:
> his right arm was caught between the belt and the
>   shaft
> and torn off at the elbow.

Accident with horse and buggy at bridge, goes over side
into stream.
Girl accused by other of theft attacks latter with razor,
cuts finger off, cuts shoulders, arms, face.
Pauper has amputation work after railway accident.
Work badly done.
Botched abortion lands woman dying in hospital.
Abortionist complains of her not keeping secret.
Man leaves wife, does not contact her despite her
putting baby's shoe, with love-note, in trunk.

Then he asked the nurse to pack his trunk,
and when the expressman came
his wife asked the man where he was going to take it
but the man would not tell her.

Just before the trunk was closed
she put in a shoe —
a little shoe, the first their baby had worn —
and put it on the tray of the trunk
and under the shoe a note:
"I married you for love;
I have lived with you for love;
and I would have clung to you for ever for love";
signed it, "Your wife,"
and addressed the note, "My husband."

Then the nurse locked the trunk
and the expressman took it away.
But she did not hear from her husband.

Stevedore falls 20 feet into hold of badly-lit coalship
lacking usual lamp at spot.
Man asks for a draw of a cigarette outside a dance;
conflict, eventual stabbing to death.
Horses drowned when they bolt on iced lake being cut
for ice-blocks.
Man leaving town hoping to kill "some son of a bitch".

His companion told him to put up his pistol:
he might hurt somebody;
and he replied that he knew how to handle a gun as
    well as any man,
and was not going to hurt anybody right there;
but added that he wanted to kill "some son of a
    bitch";
and did the man he was talking to ever feel that way?

*Father (with son's help) murders 15-year-old daughter
he had sex with, buries her in swamp.
New miner killed by cage; others didn't warn him of
the dangerous area he'd entered.
Drunk white shoots negro for refusing to put coal on
railway waiting-room fire.
Conscientious man put to new job in slaughterhouse
where platform not stationary. Falls in vat of boiling
water.
60-year-old deaf seamstress going home by night along
railroad track sucked under train.
Girl about 15 raped on way home from work at 10 p.m.;
police arrest janitor whose shoes fit snowprints.
Beating of mare.*

Several of the citizens came around,
but he told them it was his horse
and he would whip it as long as he pleased.
Every time he hit the mare, she grunted;
but she would not rear up
except when he struck her on the head.
When he stopped beating her
she had ridges on her
and the blood ran from her nostrils.

*

*Jew at Jewish office told to clean steps — with acid.
Chief Rabbi likewise. SS laugh.
8 lines about Jews forced to drink sea-water desperately*

sucking dirty water from mops and rags.
Description of the sealed-off Warsaw ghetto, with starving
people, corpses lying in streets "gnawed at by rats".
50 Jews pulled from bunker, beaten. Lined up to be shot,
order rescinded as they are to be sent away "for soap".
SS man shoots woman then rips her baby apart before her
eyes. Then gives lump of sugar to dog.
Woman picked from line undressed to be shot, told to go.
As she walks away, shot in the back.

> She took that step
> and then he said: "What a pity
> to bury such beauty in the earth.
> Go!
> But don't look backwards.
> There is the street to the boulevard.
> Follow that."
> She hesitated
> and then began to walk as told.
> The other women looked at her —
> some no doubt with envy —
> as she walked slowly, step by step.
> And the officer took out his revolver
> and shot her in the back.

Widows in Germany might be sent "Feeling well" postcard
or request for 3½ marks for urn with ashes.
Children thrown from balconies and 2nd-floor hospitals
onto trucks where sick adults lay.
Children locked up in hundreds, on way to death camps.
8-year-old keeping half a biscuit for his mother.
Dog trained to attack at word "Jew"; another called
"Man" to attack Jewish "dog".
SS man not so harsh. Moved within a month.
Jews made to stand in barrel till frozen to death. Orchestra
— reached 60 — to play whenever Jews shot.
Trucks arriving at mass graves: clothes, footwear sorted in
piles: down steps to stand on bodies: father consoling son.

The SS man at the pit,
shouted to his comrade
and he counted off twenty, now completely naked,
and told them to go down the steps cut in the clay wall
    of the pit:
here they were to climb over the heads of the dead
to where the soldier pointed.

*Hasidim led to hill to pray and raise hands for God's help.
Kerosene poured on them.
Man ordered to sort out bodies. Comes on his wife and
children. Wants to commit suicide, but escapes.
Burning of the mass graves. Grinding machine, to grind the
bones. Sieved for gold fillings.
Description of gas chamber. Bodies ripped for swallowed
jewels, hair cut for mats, "nothing to be wasted!".*

When the rear doors were opened,
those inside were standing like statues:
there had been no room to fall
or even bend.
Among the dead, families were to be seen,
holding each other by the hand,
hands tightly clasped
so that those who threw out the dead
had trouble parting them.

*

*Poland: Anno 1700. Argument between Young Jew and
Old Jew over value of nurturing historical sense of
pogroms.
Russia: Anno 1905. Address to America as goal of exiles.
Debate by "A Young Jew" as to whether or not he's
Russian.*

Or better still,
there is no Russia;
there are no peoples, only man!

*Derivation from Josephus. Pompey's soldiers at Jerusalem.
Lengthy description of gear.*

Their leather coats, heavy with bands of iron or brass,
over sleeveless woolen shirts;
a greave of bronze on the right leg –
the forwards leg in battle –
and feet in heavy sandals;
a heavy square shield of wood plated with iron
hung at each man's left. The badge of his cohort,
a bright wreath or a thunderbolt, perhaps, painted
    about the boss,
but now, on the march, under a leather cover.

*Derivation from historical record of early colonialist's
delight at Virginia.*
*Ghetto sequence. Boy who wants to learn music rather than
father's business. Leaves home. Starving.*
*Man engaged to be married. "He sang a song to himself in
which her name was the only word." Mother remonstrates
about poor health in girl's family background.*
*Shoemaker, finishing a shoe. Pot of fish on stove. Friend
waits "in shoes newly cobbled and blacked" for meal and
walk.*
*Boy ostracised by anti-semitic neighbourhood. Waits till
darkness for his sledging.*

It had been long dark, though still an hour before
    supper-time.
The boy stood at the window behind the curtain.
The street under the black sky was bluish white with
    snow.
Across the street, where the lot sloped to the pavement,
boys and girls were going down on sleds.
The boys were after him because he was a Jew.

At last his father and mother slept. He got up and
    dressed.
In the hall he took his sled and went out on tiptoe.

No one was in the street. The slide was worn smooth and
    slippery — just right.
He laid himself on his sled and shot away. He went down
    only twice.
He stood knee-deep in snow:
no one was in the street, the windows were darkened;
those near the street-lamps were ashine, but the rooms
    inside were dark;
on the street were long shadows of clods of snow.
He took his sled and went back into the house.

Mother telling son she wished she could have studied.
Collapse of a family's fortune after daughters die in child-
birth.
Autobiographical. Grandfather, his arrival from Russia, his
Hebrew words to R.'s father "I did not think to see your
face! and God has shown me your sons also." Gives R. a
Russian coin.
Schoolmates in Brooklyn. Two fellow poetry enthusiasts.
Secondhand books.
R. and friend Gabriel set themselves sonnets on given
theme, "We knew that Keats and Leigh Hunt used to do
that." Years later sees Gabriel while waiting on subway.
Gabriel looks, then looks away.
Reproof over denigration by R. of his father's buckle.

I was wearing a belt buckle
with the initial of my family name on it
in a cheap design. A friend noticed it
and I said apologetically:
"This was my father's. He had no taste."
"Perhaps," my friend answered gently,
"he wore it because it was a gift."

R.'s spell at law school. Fondness for reading, even memo-
rising law cases, "sifting the facts of each case until I had
only the hard essentials."
Gets fed up with law.

Short imagist sequences. Mainly urban. Sky stars office blocks factory girls.
Old man eating apple.

> Showing a torn sleeve, with stiff and shaking fingers
>   the old man
> pulls off a bit of the baked apple, shiny with sugar,
> eating with reverence food, the great comforter.

Address to the subway rails. The road excavation. Metropolitan haiku. The automobile fender. The traffic light jewel.

> Permit me to warn you
> against this automobile rushing to embrace you
> with outstretched fender.

*

> This smoky winter morning
> do not despise the green jewel shining among the twigs
> because it is a traffic light.

The girder "still itself among the rubbish". The lone star dogging the moon.
"The ceaseless weaving of the uneven water". The private ledger.

> Put it down in your ledger
> among the profits of this day:
> the dark uncertain path of the wind
> on the bright water;
> snow on the yellow branches of the sycamore.

Prayers. Kaddish. Te Deum.

> Not because of victories
> I sing,
> having none,
> but for the common sunshine,
> the breeze,
> the largess of the spring.

Not for victory
but for the day's work done
as well as I was able;
not for a seat upon the dais
but at the common table.

*

I've said that Reznikoff combines the here-and-now with the historic, the imagist with the narrative, and this by collocation of parts. It's not a simple matter though: it would be wrong for instance to see *Holocaust* and *Testimony* purely as examples of the narrative, historic aspect of the work. In fact it's important that each of these works is preceded by a prefatory note which states that all that follows is based on legal records. Reznikoff's getting-to-the-essentials style thus presents them in some ways as a kind of series of cleaned-up linguistic found-objects, for you to make of as you will. Again, the short here-and-now urban images of the *Complete Poems* cumulatively build up a sense of an environment, and the personality of its recorder. In fact, for all his "objective" techniques and terse diction, Reznikoff is a highly personal poet, with a strong presence throughout the poems. The bravery of his formal technique doesn't isolate him: he includes himself in the continuum that goes from the partial to the individual, to the group, to the community, to the people. He doesn't get lost. The need for food, shelter, compassion: the understanding of a Yiddish tradition he compresses to six lines.

All day the pavement has been black
with rain, but in our warm brightly-lit
room, Praise God,
I kept saying to myself,
and not saying a word,
Amen, you answered.

On the Mass Bombing of
Iraq and Kuwait,
Commonly Known as ''The Gulf War''

with

Leonard's Shorter Catechism

or

''And now would you please welcome St
Augustine of Hippo, who's come along this
evening to talk about 'The Concept of the
Just Fuel-Air-Explosive Bomb'.''

"What land has not seen Britain's crimson flag flying,
The meteor of murder, but justice the plea"

from the anonymous radical song c. 1820
"The Deluge of Carnage at length has subsided"
(See *Radical Renfrew*, pp. 90–91)

It has been a terrible six months, and more. In addition to the publicly planned and quasi-publicly executed destruction of a country and the mass murder of many of its people, there has been the extent to which the addiction of the public in Britain to the belief that they have access every hour to a source of summary about the true condition of the world – with twice-daily enlargements in print if required – has been ruthlessly exploited. It has been an essential part of the military bombing campaign: the largest bombardment of anti-language to which the British public has ever been exposed, as a necessary adjunct to its armed forces' participation in the largest military bombardment of a country in history. That bombing has stopped, but the domestic bombardment continues unchecked and apparently still unquestioned. It seems that people must not be allowed to realise the extent of the savagery that has been perpetrated in their name. By the time that the destruction of cities, towns, food-storage supplies and even essential sewage processing works does begin to dawn on the public mind, it seems it must by that time have been primed to understand that all such destruction and all such murder must be seen as the work of the demon from Hell, Saddam Hussein.

So many countries have had their eye on the carve-up to come, the backhander to be received, or the trade deal threatened with withdrawal. Amongst tonnages of printed matter and months of broadcast verbiage about morality, not a scrap of moral judgement has had any bearing on any one of the thirty or so countries involved. In the Security Council, the supposed "problem" was to have been Russia and China. But Russia is now in the soup-queue, and its handouts from Saudi Arabia and America would certainly have been scrapped with any genuine Russian opposition. China on the other hand could agree to turn a blind eye while the West reopened trade and let it get on with prosecuting the same students whose indictment for criminal offence the West had previously condemned. The phrase "all necessary means" was the core of anti-language at the heart. It meant to the Russians and the Chinese: "You three get on with the bombing, we didn't sign anything that can hold us responsible". The juxtaposition of public statement with a kind of public winking extended throughout, echoed faithfully from Bush to Major to Kinnock, and beyond. "The sole object is to drive Iraq from Kuwait": "The worst possible outcome is if Iraq now chooses to leave Kuwait". These two sentences would be used in the same paragraph as if they did not contradict each other. They didn't insofar as language was not being used honestly but strategically. It was necessary for the evasion of responsibility to say that the object of the exercise was the defence of freedom – not that freedom was a concept much known in Kuwait under the Emir. But it had to be accepted that the real object of the exercise was the effective destruction of Iraq – this for listeners of a military-strategy turn of mind. In agreeing to this understanding, the listener was flattered with a pseudo-confidentiality, and bolstered with the notion of compliance in decision-making. The decision was "not to send the wrong signals to Saddam Hussein". So certain things had to be said, and certain things had to be understood. Mum's the word, corporal.

The BBC World Service in its broadcasts to North America often focuses on the transactions taking place in the United Nations building in New York. On March 20th – which happens to be the day this article is being written – the 3 a.m. news announced the report of the United Nations envoy to Iraq. The envoy had travelled extensively in the country, and found a major and "dramatic" – to quote the adjective used – cause for world concern. Iraq is devastated, with roads and means of communications destroyed. There is a desperate shortage of food throughout the country. The agricultural system has broken down due to the failure of fuel supplies which, like the food storage containers, have been destroyed by the bombing. The price of corn is already beyond the reach of most Iraqis. There are thousands of refugees fleeing into Iran, into an area already devastated by the Iran–Iraq war. Many of these people, women, children, and men, are suffering from the burn effects of Allied – the report specifically said "Allied" – bombing. They are not receiving proper medical treatment. There is a chronic shortage of medicine as well as food for Iraqis, and with the coming hot weather the risk of plague is increasing. The pressure should grow, the report concluded, for the Secretary General to reconvene the Security Council in order to ask that the embargo on food and medicine into Iraq – which has now operated for seven months – should be lifted.

None of these details are themselves new or surprising. Anyone who has not wilfully shut out the thought of what must be the effect of blocking food and medicine to 17½ million people for months, then dropping 2,500 planeloads of bombs on their country every day for seven weeks, would not require an envoy from the United Nations to warn them of a human disaster. All the horrors of so-called "conventional" weapons that had been stored up in Germany for use against the Communists have been dropped on a conscript and civilian population. The people who had suffered for more than twenty years under a dictator whom the West had propped up over them, now have had to suffer many times worse the murder and terror for which he had been responsible; but the new murder and terror was from the "Allies" – which is to say principally America, Britain and France. Nothing short of nuclear weapons was spared, and these were spared both because the effects could be otherwise achieved, and because their use would have been counter-productive in propaganda terms. The "fuel-air-explosive" bombs used are sometimes artfully described, in their capacity to incinerate everything within a radius of several miles, as each being "equivalent to a tactical nuclear weapon". Napalm was used, though when this story broke, and instantly disappeared, it was not before assurances that it was "only being used on ditches filled with petrol". The burns of the refugees arriving in Iran are burns from napalm.

And the devastation was inflicted not only on Iraq but on Kuwait itself, which was supposed to be being "liberated". Several days before the final conflagration, a Press briefing boasted of "more than 3,000" bomber attacks on Kuwait over two days alone. Again this was hardly surprising. The Emir himself had said that if it was necessary to flatten Kuwait in order to "liberate" it, this is what should be done. A reporter phoning in to Irish radio – which was one station where one could occasionally hear reports that hadn't been cleared by the "Allied" censors – described his feelings when from a helicopter near the Kuwait border he first saw the dense black clouds on the horizon of the oil wells on fire: "We thought at first it was just another massive Allied air-raid." Another reporter described how from thirty miles within the Saudi Arabian border the ground was shaking under his feet from the force of the bombs landing across the Kuwaiti border, where the whole sky was lit up with flashes. This long before the so-called "turkey shoot" of the retreating Iraqi forces, which apparently caused some public figures such surprise and anguish. One report in the *Guardian* midway through the "war" mentioned US pilots' reluctance to knock off for sleep because they wanted to be over Kuwait and Iraq bombing, the targets were so easy. There was practically an air-traffic jam, apparently, and as there was no resistance from the Iraqi airforce, which had simply fled, bombing runs could add insult to injury by not even bothering to switch off their undercarriage lights. This report was unusual in that the *Guardian*, like all the newspapers, quality or tabloid, remained wholly jingoistic throughout the campaign. The *Observer*, like many of the "qualities", found time to praise Mr Major's "tone". Now one knows what tone should be adopted by a British prime minister when his troops are firing Cruise Missiles into civilian cities.

It is logical to Western governments that no Arab country should be allowed to control oil supplies unless it is sympathetic to Western perceived needs. The countries involved, including Iraq and Kuwait, were the invention of Western diplomats earlier this century. The discovery of oil has meant the monarchy card has had to be played with a vengeance, giving spurious historical validity to these new entities whilst being cheaper to maintain than a permanent foreign standing army. So cordial diplomatic relations have been necessary with "families" who seem to spend one half of their lives breeding children of the same surname and the other half breeding horses or sitting at gaming tables. British domestic policies – such as the Labour government turn-around of 1976 – have had to be adjusted to suit such as the Emir of Kuwait's investment plans. Shuttlings between the palaces of either country have been a crucial part of protocol. The nub and only relevance is the contractual linking to British and American oil company interests. One newspaper report before the bombing started noted how the Kuwaiti minister of defence – one of the ruling Al Sabah family of course – had lost more at the gaming tables in Monte Carlo the previous week than his régime spent in health care in a whole year. The same report noted that amongst the first industries to be affected by Kuwaiti destabilisation would be the British horse-racing industry. These were the people whose régime the young working-class soldiers from the housing schemes of Britain had to be sent to "defend".

But once the "war" got under way such criticism by newspapers was abandoned, and one and all lined up behind Queen and Country. This included the Glasgow *Evening Times*, for instance, which the day before the bombing began had carried an opinion poll showing 70% of Scottish people against military action. The best that can be said about papers like the *Evening Times* is that at least they weren't openly racist like the morning tabloids. One knew what to expect from Mr Maxwell's organs: he publicly stated, at a "Solidarity with Israel" conference in 1989, that newspapers should not attack the Israeli government nor publish "rubbish" such as the intelligence report which claimed genuine Israeli–Palestinian negotiations must mean talking to the PLO. The headline in one of his newspapers before Christmas – "Crazed Arab Stabs Scots Squaddie" – is more or less par for the Middle-Eastern course from his *Daily Record* and *Sunday Mail*. One might go on here about the anti-Arab racism that has been such a prominent feature of American culture this past decade and more – e.g. in numerous simple things like the mindless "terrorists" in the otherwise excellent "Back to the Future" film by Spielberg – but this would require another article. It is just another twist in the story of anti-Semitism: people tend to forget that both the Arabic and the Jewish peoples are Semitic.

Besides the Press the main source of "information" has been the daily "briefings" by various Army representatives, and the reports on television and radio subject to Ministry of Defence control in conjunction with the public relations firm hired by John Wakeham to sell the conduct of the "war" on the government's behalf. Walking along a main road past shops selling banked rows of televisions in Britain during January and February 1991, was like being in South America, El Salvador or Chile. At any hour of the day these shop windows would be filled with images of a person in a flak jacket dispensing solemn "information" to wholly subservient and unprobing journalists. The image that occurs about what actually took place at these "briefings" is one that I think comes from Karl Kraus, about a music-hall sketch in which on stage a streetlamp casts a small circle of light. Around is total darkness. A man has dropped a sixpence, and he spends his time walking round and round the lamp-post, looking for his sixpence in the circle of light. That to me was what the "briefings" were about. Many words were taboo, chief of which was the word "Iraq" itself. The possibility had to be avoided that people might actually imagine a real country with real people having an ancient culture. Instead there was the language-bombardment of demonology: "Saddam" this, "Saddam" that — as if it was a personal demon that was stretched like Gulliver from Turkey to Saudi Arabia. As for the catalogue of horrors that was being dropped on this demon's territory, there was a tension between the wish to brag about the efficacy of its mayhem and the need not to let people's mental pictures of this mayhem become graphic and actual. Thus what was bragged of as the biggest aerial bombardment in the history of warfare somehow became bound up with its also being one of the greatest acts of humanitarian charity the world had ever seen. As Mr Bush in one of his many incredible black=white statements put it, the whole operation was "a victory for the human race". It seemed at one point as if the designer of the Cruise missile would be in line for this year's Nobel Prize for Peace. Here were thousand-pound bombs that seemingly paused at the kerb to let old ladies cross the road. And the gentlemen of the Press marvelled, wrote it down, and showed it on television. After all, it fell well within the light cast by the streetlamp on the stage.

But the most crucial part in the conduct of the "war" at home has been played neither by the Press nor by the broadcasting companies, but by Parliament, in particular the parties of Opposition. The polls such as were allowed to be published before January 17th showed deep division of opinion in the country. If Parliament had reflected that division, if the Opposition parties had reflected the huge opposition there was to military intervention, then the effect would have been very significant. Broadcasts would have had to have reflected the Parliamentary divisions, as would have the Press. But the tabloids would probably have screamed Treason, and that is probably the main reason why, just as at the time of the

Falklands Adventure, Labour decided that the only possible course was to enter wholeheartedly into a *de facto* Government of National Unity. "Politics" were suspended. If one called up the "Politics" or "Parliament" sections on Ceefax, there was for weeks virtually nothing there, other than a few directions to which pages contained Gulf War "information". In the Commons itself, the exchanges between Major and Kinnock became ever more affable, ever more "statesman-like". Labour's foreign minister, Kaufmann, seemed almost to speak slower and a little deeper than usual, as if he had had tuition from the same How-to-Sound-Grave-and-Important tutor as has trained Douglas Hurd. The main activity for the Shadow front bench was to minimise "revolt" in the Parliamentary Party. This meant that Healey could express his opposition to the War so long as he didn't actually vote with Benn against it. Other MPs could be seen having their own cake and eating it in this fashion, with or without articles by such as Brian Wilson in the *Glasgow Herald*. It was left to a small bunch loosely though not entirely associated with Benn who consistently expressed their opposition, and voted accordingly; people like George Galloway and Maria Fyfe. Each expression of humanitarian principle, each crumb of sanity, had to be seized on with gratitude. The Pope and the Catholic hierarchy in Scotland, the Protestant World Council of Churches, the Moderator of the Church of Scotland – all shamed those politicians who couldn't even find within themselves the humanitarianism of the official orthodox clergy. The grotesqueries of a "thanksgiving service" is a political move to cover some of these tracks.

And what of the Scottish National Party? After all, it was Scotland which expressed 70% opposition on the eve of the bombing's commencement. Unfortunately if the Parliamentary Labour Party can be fairly understood as having stifled mass opposition throughout the UK to the "war" once it got under way, in Scotland this can be even more pointedly said of the SNP. They it is who have spoken about Labour's abandonment of the socialist and working-class vote in Scotland, an abandonment they have recently claimed to seek to make good. But the various wings of the SNP hadn't a clue what to say about the "war" other than make pathetic mutterings about percentages of Jocks versus Sassenachs at the front. When it came to the most important decision of foreign policy since the Second World War, yet again the SNP was tied to its "your-liege-Ma'am, bonny-fechters-the-warld-ower" camp followers; people whose idea of a liberated Scotland is the Royal Toast given in Lallans. But the SNP, like some on the so-called "soft left" of the Parliamentary Labour Party, did make some protest about "staying within United Nations guidelines". This meant not actually invading Iraq. At present Iraq has not only been invaded, it has an army of occupation, and many thousands of bodies have had to be cleared. However, that is a taboo subject, and no-one is asking any questions about it – neither the SNP nor the Labour Party. For the truth is that though the mass bombing has stopped, reporting is still firmly under the control of the Ministry of Defence. Any bodies, any destruction, any disease, is to be blamed on Hussein and the present civil war over which the Allies have booked rather more than a grandstand seat. The British parliamentary parties have been very glad of the opportunity provided by the Budget to re-enter at last the theatre of oppositional dialogue. It is as if the Speaker had blown a ceremonial whistle for the ritual once more to begin. What better than with the annual pantomime of the Budget – that yearly ceremonial-encumbered ritual tinkering with tax, fags and booze which shuns the really dirty work such as the raising of prescription charges that is pushed through on other days without studio discussion, elaborate presentation or response? But at any rate with the Budget, Parliament can now be declared officially "back to normal".

Normality in reporting from the Gulf though remains total censorship. Having listened to the BBC World Service 3 a.m. news, I was still awake at 5.30, so watched the ITV "World News" broadcast that goes out then. There was again a special report from Iraq, quite a few minutes long. It made no mention of the United Nations envoy's report. It did mention fighting between Iraqi government forces and Kurds, and it mentioned refugees fleeing into Iran – refugees burned with napalm. However by omission the clear message was that these were people who had been napalmed by Hussein's forces. As for Kuwait, there was still no report on the massive damage done by "Allied" bombing, and there was still no report on how many oilwells were on fire. This information the Army Command has been refusing to supply, perhaps because it might seem too much like a "propaganda coup" for "the enemy", or too obviously a fulfilment of the "ecological disaster" forewarned by many who opposed military action. However the problem of discussing it best has to be faced, and the report of 5.30 a.m. made some start. It showed children and elderly people in hospitals with respiratory problems, whose conditions have been exacerbated by the blanket of oil-thick smog over Kuwait City. How refreshing it was to hear British anxiety over the provision of medicine to the young and the elderly in the region. What a difference a border makes. And the British soldiers were conspicuously solicitous too. There were unexploded mines lying around Kuwait, and a group of British soldiers were filmed making a television advert warning children how to recognise them, and not to touch them. So the combined sequence of quite typical icons from this "report from the Gulf", three weeks after the bombing has stopped, gave this message: "Saddam Hussein is waging war on children and old people by air and ground. The British serviceman is doing his best to protect the people from this." As for the United Nations report – not a word.

These news bulletins on this particular day, March 20th 1991, are unusual only insofar as it was possible at 3 a.m. to hear a report highly critical of the "Allies" in respect of the total destruction and the continuing suffering caused by them in Iraq. The 9 a.m. BBC Radio Four bulletin six hours later was, like the ITV news, wholly uncritical. Its only Middle East report was that the Kuwaiti cabinet had resigned. People were fed up that there was still no electricity and other supplies – apparently there had been much sabotage done by the Iraqis before they left. Of damage done by British and American bombing – again not a word. There has been no mention of that since the bombing stopped, other than an occasional reference to the "battle for building contracts" that the government minister Peter Lilley will be flying out to wage with some business friends.

The deliberate destruction of a country, of its means of communications and of its population's means of maintaining life and health; the deliberate refusal to consider peace terms until as many as possible of a conscript army has been exterminated using weapons against which they have no means of defending themselves: this to me is an act of genocide. But this word causes disquiet about exaggeration or dramatisation, not least because people feel you can't use the same word for the murder of six million people as you use for much lesser amounts. I have looked up the United Nations convention on genocide; some might argue for the term "political mass murder" in this case. If so, let them call it that. How many were murdered might never be known: the American commander in charge has said he is "not in the business of body counts". Neither is President Hussein. One would have thought that it might have at least occurred to people that there will be Iraqi survivors, or their descendants, who will feel that if there is any justice in the world, the cities of Britain and America will one day get at least a little of what their citizens were apparently so indifferent to inflicting on the towns and cities of Iraq.

To let one's mind continue in turmoil over present enormities is to reduce oneself effectively to the status of a Francis Bacon scream. The enormities have at no time in history been absent from a fully defined contemporary context of any single happy human life. There's a maturity of maturity, the crossing point where you decide not to go "insane" but to insist on your own indestructible – except through death – status as a human being and a citizen of the world. Accepting this is to accept the always present validity of humour and dalliance, of turning up the road to the left or wherever because that's what briefly occurs, to sit somewhere out of anyone's planned cognizance looking at the lines in your hand, or a leaf, or the sky for no other reason than because there is no reason to do so. That is nothing to do with "sentimentality" in my opinion. It is to do with being a human being.

The following "Questions and Answers on the Gulf War" were completed at the time of the end of the bombing on February 28th. I called them *Leonard's Shorter Catechism*, or "*And now would you please welcome St Augustine of Hippo, who's come along this evening to talk about 'The Concept of the Just Fuel-Air-Explosive Bomb'.*"

Q What is meant by the phrase "by peaceful means"?

A "By peaceful means" is a special United Nations phrase meaning "No food or medicine to be allowed in" to a country. If for instance Iraq, Palestine, and Cuba had a disagreement with Great Britain and were able to blockade the country from receiving any food or medicine, this would be called "pursuing their disagreement with Great Britain by peaceful means".

Q Why did Pope Urban the Second launch the First Crusade?

A "To restore peace and stability in the Middle East".

Q Who said "Blessed are the meek: for they shall inherit the earth"?

A This was said by Jesus Christ on the Mount of Olives. He was quoting in anticipation George Bush, who used the words in his address to the American people after ordering the mass bombing of Iraq.

Q What flies from Gloucestershire?

A This might be any one of a number of migratory birds of Gloucestershire which winter in the Mediterranean or Africa. For example, the Garden Warbler, the Nightjar, the Swift, the Stonechat, or the Whinchat with its snappy *tic-tac* and soft *peu*, and its 5–7 pale blue eggs laid in a cupped surface on the ground under shrubbery.

Q   What do you call something that flies from Gloucestershire to a place where it "minces everything on the ground within an area one mile wide by three miles long"?

A   A human being.

Q   What do you call the things that mince everything on the ground within an area one mile wide by three miles long?

A   "Conventional weapons".

Q   **What flies across France?**

A   Only birds, planes, human beings and conventional weapons are allowed to fly across France.

Q   **Sphinx: What goes on four legs in the morning, two legs in the afternoon, and three legs in the evening?**

A   American pilot: "A cockroach".

Q   **What is the percentage of people in command of the British Army who have working-class accents?**

A   I'm sorry, he *would* have been pleased to speak to you, but he is in bed with laryngitis.

Q   **What is the percentage of British troops in the front line who have public-school accents?**

A   I'm sorry, he *would* have been pleased to speak to you, but he is in bed with laryngitis.

Q   **What do you get after three weeks if you lock a million-and-a-half people up for 24 hours a day?**

A   Thirteen billion dollars.

Q   **What did the Scottish National Party say when Iraq annexed Kuwait?**

A   "It's Scotland's oil!"

Q   **Pete asks: "If Marconi invented the radio, and Winston**

Churchill invented Kuwait, who invented the steam engine?"

A   James Watt. And he was Scottish.

Q   What is the etymology of the words "Saudi Arabia"?

A   "Saudi Arabia" is an abbreviation from an ancient Arabic phrase which translates literally as "The Aramco Oil Company International".

Q   In which book does Biggles have a dogfight with the Airforce of the World Enemy, thus helping to save the world at great personal risk?

A   *Biggles Goes to War*, *Biggles Flies South*, *Biggles Flies North*, etc.

Q   In which book does the Airforce of the World Enemy run away, so Biggles bombs cities, towns, roads, bridges, telephone exchanges, water supplies and electricity supplies, so that the survivors have difficulty getting food and the injured have difficulty getting treatment?

A   *The Minutes of the British War Cabinet January–February 1991.*

Q   What did the Labour Shadow Cabinet say when it realised it was an essential part of a Government of National Unity waging planned genocide?

A   Shhh.

Q   What did you used to call someone who should feel guilty about their country's past policy of genocide?

A   A German.

Q   What do you call a quarter of a million Germans marching in 1991 against genocide?

A   "Anti-semitic".

Q   What do you do when a president gasses 5,000 people in his own country?

A   Show the bodies on television – but keep selling him arms.

Q   What do you do when a president's troops invade Panama killing another 5,000 people?

A   Don't show the bodies on television.

Q   What does "control of the airwaves" mean?

A   It means suspending oil adverts until people can watch them and keep their food down at the same time.

A   The telephones sell-off, the gas sell-off, the water sell-off, the electricity sell-off, the Tory leadership contest, the total destruction of Iraq . . .

Q   What is the question?

Q   What did Britain take part in on Tuesday, February 19th 1991?

A   It took part in what was at that point "one of the most ferocious attacks on the centre of Baghdad", using bombers and Cruise Missiles fired from ships.

Q   What did John Major say about the bombing the next day?

A   He said: "One is bound to ask about attacks such as these: What sort of people is it that can carry them out? They certainly are consumed with hate. They are certainly sick of mind, and they can be certain of one thing – they will be hunted and hunted until they are found."
(He was talking about 5lb of explosive left in a litter-bin at Victoria Station in London. This killed one person and critically injured three.)

Q   "Many of these modern weapons show a considerable amount of imagination in their construction. I was told the other day that some rockets can each saturate an area the size of 60 football pitches. Is this true?"

A   "Yes! They're fired from multiple-rocket-launch systems, and twelve can be fired at a time. Every rocket breaks up into 600 smaller bombs or "bomblets" before they land. They're sometimes jocularly called "the honourable members" after the honourable members of the British House of Commons that voted for the war. You could maybe have a think about *that* next time you're watching Prime Minister's Question Time on TV!"

Q   **What does "I will only continue to support the war if it stays within United Nations guidelines" mean?**

A   It means "I support the mass bombing and total destruction of Iraq but I do not support the sending in of armed human beings."

Q   **What does United Nations Resolution 242 state?**

A   Shhh.

Q   **What do you do with wee babies, four-year-olds, five-year-olds, grannies, people whom you would get on with fine if you knew them, people who would get on your nerves, football supporters, teachers, tradesmen, shop-keepers, writers, unemployed people, people that work with their hands, people that work with pens or comput-ers, janitors, directors of firms, managers, people that work at home, bus drivers, taxi drivers, actors, electri-cians, policemen, clergy, workaholics, feckless wasters, boys out of school into uniform, older soldiers, musi-cians, alcoholics, geniuses, idiots, people who don't like the light being turned off at night, people who "prefer the old ways", people who whistle in the street?**

A   Ehm. . . What country are they from?

(*et cetera, ad infinitum*)

nora's place

across the park, walking
I can't be bothered
making the dinner, going through
all the routines and subroutines

setting it up with the radio at
four to do the peeling, work out
what the rota's been of

food this past week or so
is it time again for fish

trying to get the girls
not eat before dinner
when they come in from school

I protest at this place
with no people in it

objects for reproducing images
people not actually present

from this wall to this wall
and this wall to this wall

yes I'm all for him
becoming union rep
– don't let them get away with it!

obviously   the last settlement
was a complete sell-out
                              but then,
aren't most union leaders like that?

on the executive, hobnobbing
far too much with managers
                              first-name terms
                              and they're always
paid far more than the worst off
who need the union most

Dives and Lazarus
that's what we agreed
last night at dinner time

soon it will be
the familiar footsteps
time   sometimes from the

bottom of the stairs the
voices drift up   maybe

if you happen to look out the window
at the right time, it is the right time

for a wave.   the wave.
people are coming home.
                              home to

the place that has not existed
these past hours

if they're finding

the dinner school portions too wee it
must be the cutbacks that'll mean
they'd better come home at

the back of half twelve every
day I'll better maybe
keep a big pot of soup on the

go or get in some
frozen packets hamburgers
fish fingers that sort of thing

you can't give them
chips twice a day though it
wouldn't be a healthy

diet maybe I'll try to
get them go back to dinner school
take pieces with them though

to eke it out

I don't know what we share exclusively now
other than the children

the best time was when we shared the same political outlook
exclusively   but now

you've others you can do that with
the shared anger at injustice
can be had elsewhere

the main thing to have controlled
contempt for the idea of
breakdown which is completely

unromantic and painful despite
its aura and pseudo visionary crap about
insights usually obsessive petty

vanities to do with god and the
devil and one-dimensional trains
of thought that go on and on and

people don't understand you any better
at the end of it

through the
revolving turnstile
past

tomatoes
mushrooms   peppers
potatoes

cheese island
milk   margarine
yoghurt

pizzas jams marmalades
beans peas carrots
pulses   sauces

coffee tea
spaghetti
hoops spam   tuna

salmon
ambrosia creamed rice
soups

cornflakes
all bran shredded
wheat   fruit

juice soda stream
cooking oil
disposable bin liners

124

brillo dettol
washing soda crystals
elastoplast toothpaste

kleenex toilet rolls
soap powders fairy
liquid

dog food
birds eye codsteaks
hamburgers

frozen turkey
chicken
new zealand lamb

biscuit alley
fresh fish
on the spot baking

stand
leaning on the trolley
waiting

nora drinks too much

sometimes one beer is enough to make her go
what is it about nora's drinking

nora creates an environment in which she is approved
if she sits with drinkers, her being a drinker is approved
she is "finally approved simply for what she is"

nora is allowed out the house twice a week
nora's terms are that she doesn't sit with males
nora doesn't want to sit with males anyway
nora sits with alice and betty, who are always there

when nora gets to the Whistler's Dog, alice and betty
                                    approve of her coming

now he has an affair of the soul elsewhere
now he has the chance to be "as free as himself"
that is what it's about, the sense to be "as free as himself"

maybe to be as free as himself, he has to have the mother
                                                    at home

                              *

when will nora become herself
when will nora feel "as free as herself"

is nora "just another person"?

you get that way you get
scared to go out –
                    don't you:

just that way that
you find yourself putting off
going to the butchers or
                    the newsagents;

that thing about
                    just talking,
where do you put your eyes:
where do you put your eyes
when you're
                    just talking?

people can tell when you're
                    not good at it, look

surprised and a bit hurt

lying looking sideways up
at the bedside photo of my youngest

strange to see that smile
that same set of features
on the face of a woman of fifty

looking back into the room
on an occasion I will never know

long after I'm dead

out there
in sexual space

deep in the darkness
breath and rhythm

moving to join
into our orb

how quirky I am
but

I'm not a table
or a pen
or a hill

I'm just a human being
totally representative
as anyone is
outside the self

(and in it)

I wish you would touch me more
it makes me feel happy
and secure

here she comes,
                 down the stairs
slowly, shopping bag in hand

trying not to think
of the heart-beat, the shallow speed
of the breathing

do you listen to your breath

who on earth
tries to control their breath
on their way to the shops

nora's place nora's

nora's place   place nora's place

nora's place   nora's place nora's

nora's place   place nora's place

nora's place

nora's place   nora's place nora's

nora's place   place nora's place

nora's place

nora's place   nora's place nora's

nora's place   place nora's place

nora's place   nora's place   nora's place nora's place

nora's place   nora's place   nora's place nora's place   nora's place nora's

nora's place   nora's place   nora's place nora's place   place nora's place

nora's place nora's

place nora's place

            nora's place nora's place
            nora's place nora's place
            nora's place nora's place

only this particular
street to walk the length

of, this
is not a metaphor, only

being suddenly
walking down a street

in this place, having
this particular sense
not of anxiety, but

"the fact of the presence of existence"

                    *

each time it happens
it seems

that all the intervening times
have disappeared

and this
is all that nora really is

ANTIDOTES ANECDOTES & ACCUSATIONS: SATIRICAL, PERSONAL AND POLITICAL PIECES 1982–94

Some of these pieces were published as *Satires and Profanities* by the Scottish Trade Union Congress during the miners' strike of 1984.

A few were issued as a pamphlet by the Edward Polin Press, printed by Clydeside Press in 1990.

"A Letter on Being Asked to Contribute to an Anthology" was first published by Infolio in 1993 under the title "A Letter in Reply to a Request for a poem for a *Poems for Bosnia* anthology, 'in which *The Independent* has an interest'."

Some notes about the pieces appear at the back of the book.

BBC News 1982

ANNOUNCER: This is the nine o'clock news.

The Russians are our enemies. They are an evil race of scheming little moustachioed bastards, who lie awake at night counting the countries they wish to invade. In the morning they get up and invade them. They do not go to church. They are at their most devious when they are not invading people. They should be expunged from the face of the earth.

Our Russian Affairs correspondent has the details.

1ST EXPERT: The Russians are our enemies. They are an evil race of scheming little moustachioed bastards, who lie awake at night counting the countries they wish to invade. In the morning they get up and invade them. They do not go to church. They are at their most devious when they are not invading people. They should be expunged from the face of the earth.

ANNOUNCER: A new "Infant Opportunities Programme" was announced today by Mr Norman Tebbit, the Employment Minister. It is designed to take the strain off sorely-pressed Local Authorities, at present spending lavish sums of ratepayers' money on the provision of urban nursery schools. Infants will be given useful clerical employment in Job Centres and Social Security offices, and it is hoped that by 1993 all staff presently employed in these departments will have been replaced by people between the ages of 3 and 5. The "Eye-Ops" as they will be called, will

work a 72-hour week, for a weekly salary of two tubes of Smarties and a Mars Bar.
Mr Tebbit later denied that his family have substantial shareholdings in Rowntree Mackintosh Limited.

The South Africans are our kith and kin. They are white, comfortably off, own their own homes, speak pretty good English and don't like Blacks. On Sundays they all get up and go to Church. On Saturdays they all get up and go play cricket. Mondays to Fridays they work pretty damned hard and deserve every kruger they earn. They hold no truck with trade unions. They are a bastion against Marxism. Our Southern Africa correspondent has the details.

2ND EXPERT: The South Africans are our kith and kin. They are white, comfortably off, own their own homes, speak pretty good English and don't like Blacks. On Sundays they all get up and go to Church. On Saturdays they all get up and go play cricket. Mondays to Fridays they work pretty damned hard and deserve every kruger they earn. They hold no truck with trade unions. They are a bastion against Marxism.

ANNOUNCER: Mr Tony Benn has denied a report in today's *Daily Mail* that he is the organiser of a "flash and run" campaign by militant left-wing extremists in the National Union of Mineworkers. The report, which has been handed to the Director of Public Prosecutions, alleges that Mr Benn has been organising coachloads of "flying flashers" to visit the homes of disabled and handicapped old ladies throughout Britain.
Mr Benn, a member of the National Executive of the Labour Party, has recently been congratulated on the size of his moustache. He suffers from insomnia.
And now for this evening's report from El Salvador.

(*Silence for 10 seconds.*)

Our El Salvador correspondents have the details.

1ST EXPERT: (*Silence for 10 seconds.*)

2ND EXPERT: (*Silence for 10 seconds.*)

ANNOUNCER: Makes you think . . .

But now for tonight's concluding story about our friendly security forces, a furry animal, and a member of the Royal Family. This is the point where we give you an amusing little anecdote to cheer you up before hitting you between the eyes with a farewell summary of the propagandist shite.
Are you sitting comfortably? Then I'll begin.
The Fire Brigade was called to Buckingham Palace today after the Queen Mother had issued a statement that a dead cat was stuck up the Duke of Edinburgh's arse. Mrs Barbara Woodhouse, who had twice failed in an attempt to breathe up its nose —

VOICE: C U T !

Rangers Sign the
Pope

(*Alex enters, brandishing a copy of the* Evening Times)

ALEX: Heh Wullie! Rangers huv signed the Pope!

WULLIE: Whut?

ALEX: Rangers huv signed the Pope! It's oan the back page! Listen tay this.

(*Reads*)

> Ibrox supremo Jock Wallace silenced his critics this morning when he emerged from behind closed doors to announce that Glasgow Rangers have signed the head of the Roman Catholic church, His Holiness Pope John Paul the Second. Denying that the signing had any religious significance, Mr Wallace said that the Pontiff's gritty tackling, his intelligent running off the ball, and his flair for the unexpected box-to-box defensive break, had been one of the most closely guarded Vatican secrets of post-war years. For his part, the Pope was reported to be "over the moon" at the speed with which the hush-hush deal had been clinched. The Papal jet is expected to fly out from Rome this evening in time for the Holy Father to take the field in tomorrow's all-important tussle with Kilmarnock at Rugby Park.

WULLIE: Whut huv they signed the Pope fur? When did he last kick a baw? He's ancient!

ALEX: Naw, it's good tay huv an auld heid in the defence Wullie. Look at Ronnie Simpson wi Celtic. Ah think they'll use the Pope as a sub.

WULLIE: Yi canny bring the Pope oan as a sub – yi'd huv tay kerry im oan in a chair!

ALEX: He'll be wearing the red-white-and-blue, Wullie. There's naibdy gets kerried aboot in a chair wearing the red-white-and-blue.

WULLIE: Aye right enough. Dae yi think he'll turn?

ALEX: The Pope?

WULLIE: Aye.

ALEX: Naw – no right away anyway. He'll no turn afore the Kilmarnock gemm, it widny look right. It'd look as if Rangers hud pit the pressure oan him.

WULLIE: Spoil the effect, aye. They'd need tay go lookin fur another wan. An they'll no get another Pope in a hurry!

ALEX: Stull. Ah think they've the heid screwed oan. There's wan problem Rangers'll no huv wi His Holiness Pope John Paul the Second.

WULLIE: Whut's that Alex?

ALEX: At least he wullny marry a Catholic!

Scotland Today

The paddle-steamer *Waverley* received a tumultuous reception at Glasgow's Broomielaw today, on its return from active service in the Falklands. The *Waverley* was requisitioned last year during a mystery tour off Dunoon, and despatched to the South Atlantic with a morale-boosting cargo of several tons of gaily-coloured seaside rock.

On deck waving back to the cheering crowds were the Scottish country dance bands who had worked a 24-hour rota shift throughout the entire campaign. Falklands veterans have testified to the heroism of the gallant paddle-steamer which, from the landing at San Carlos to the taking of Stanley, stood just half a mile offshore, pouring out a continuous medley of reels and strathspeys.

The ship's captain will tomorrow be presented with the freedom of Millport, and it is hoped that later this month he will lead the welcoming party on the return from the South Atlantic of the Govan Ferry.

Mr Endrews Speaks

The following scene takes place in St Kevin Barry's, a large school in Glasgow. Over the tannoy, which has speakers in every classroom, comes the voice of Mr Andrews, the new headmaster. He speaks with a Kelvinside accent.

*

This is your headmester speaking. This is Mr Endrews, your new headmester. I want to make one thing clear above all. It is my determination to make St Kevin Berry's a school of which the city of Glesgow cen be justly proud. This city of Glesgow, the envy of Europe for its many beautiful perks.

Why only the other day in one of these beautiful perks, Kelvingrove, I chenced across a former pupil of this very school, who enswered to the name of "Tem". Now Tem, I could see, was thinking long thoughts over a small bottle of hair lecquer. Beside him on his bench lay one of his unfortunate pels, who hed some hours before shaken off this mortal coil. Rigor mortis was complete, end his right hend was set in what is known es "a messonic hendshake". "Tem," I said severely, hev you been freternising with those of enother faith?" But Tem slid forward from his bench, end went to join his hepless friend in thet lend from whose bourn, no treveller returns.

Now Tem was never one to hev known the dignity of a laudable profession with a substential celery, like my own. It was his own fault, of course. Et St Kevin Berry's he would hev the school motto, Porridge end the Tawse, inscribed on all his

Eff Two's. But a leck of self-discipline was to prove his downfall in later years. You know, my feather was gerrotted when I was a child end it didn't do *me* any herm. No, I stuck herd et my studies, end in the fullness of time became a greduate of Glasgow University. End there were no state hendouts in my day; one hed to get by on a seck of oats. (*Clears his throat*) A seck of oats.

Of course none of you listening to me here this morning will ever go to Glasgow University, I'm aware of thet. Most of you will be in the hends of the Glasgow Constebulary before very long, end some of you will no doubt make your appearance in the High Court on a cherge of murder. Now I want you to hev the honour of St Kevin Berry's in mind when you plead guilty, end under no circumstences should you use the glottal stop. I want you all to say "Guilty", in a clear, well-mennered voice, with no trace of slovenly speech.

Teachers. Efter this address, all clesses will prectise saying "Guilty" for thirty minutes. Tomorrow morning et 9 a.m. sherp I will make a rendom inspection, end any boy who uses the glottal stop in reply to my question, "How do you plead?" will be for six of the belt. With my new Lochgelly, which can stend on its own.

Finally. You will no doubt be aware thet with the coming of Spring, it is no longer derk between the hours of four end five. This means thet I will be doubly severe with those pupils caught urinating in the hedges of local gerdens on the way home from school. If pupils behave like seveges, they will be sevegely dealt with.

Now I want Thomas Maguire end Frencis Lawson of Four Zed in my office et once. Sherp.

Beer Advert

(A man, clutching a pint of beer)

Hi there, fellas.

You know, a few years ago, I used to have this daft idea that maybe some women might find my penis a bit on the small side.

That I'd go to bed with some chick, and she'd just tell me it was too *wee*. It really used to screw me up – you can imagine.

I think it was this stuff that saved me. Younger's Tartan Special. It's got a full body. It satisfies. And it really attacks your thirst.

These days, if ever I spot a chick I'd *really* like to hit the sack with, I just order up half-a-dozen pints of Younger's Tartan Special.

And I go and get pished.

Hawdyir Scrotum: A Young Conservative Philosopher

JOAN: Last week "Options" interviewed the grey eminence of the Labour Movement, Sir Hector McKellar. Tonight I have with me one of the most innovative and frankly spoken of the new breed of radical Conservatives – the Right Honourable Hawdyir Scrotum.

SCROTUM: Good evening.

JOAN: Mr Scrotum, you have received an amount of criticism recently for your statement that headmasters of comprehensive schools should be armed with Thompson submachine guns, automatic rifles, and be allowed to patrol the streets of their local communities.

SCROTUM: Well, up here in Scotland I find a strange mixture of fear and respect for headmasters. They seem such remote figures in the public mind – as rare as ospreys to spot. I think it's time we persuaded them to adopt a higher profile, to come out from behind their walnut desks. You know, armed headmasters on patrol would take a tremendous strain off our security forces.

JOAN: But surely the unions wouldn't buy it?

SCROTUM: Oh the headmasters in the unions would, there'd be no problem there. "Responsibility payments" – those are the magic words. Walk into a headmasters' meeting and whisper "responsibility payments": all their little eyes light up like Blackpool illuminations.

161

JOAN: But surely we can't have children being gunned down in the streets by men in mortarboards and gowns?

SCROTUM: Oh there would be no reason for anyone to fear anything like that: there would be a very strict enforcement of the "warning card" procedure. Only if a pupil pointedly refused to halt when called on to do so by his headmaster, would that headmaster be permitted to open fire.

JOAN: But if this system would be as foolproof as you maintain, why do you also propose that teachers be issued with plastic bullets?

SCROTUM: I prefer that you call them plastic rounds.

JOAN: But I always think of plastic rounds as being sort of open sandwiches, full of processed cheese.

SCROTUM: Precisely. That's why I prefer that you call them plastic rounds.

JOAN: All right then. Why do you propose that teachers be issued with "plastic rounds"?

SCROTUM: Three reasons, in the main. One, because teachers now have to adapt the curriculum to the phasing out of corporal punishment. Two, to facilitate speedier integration of the child into the big world beyond the playground gates. And three, because Mr and Mrs Joe Public are not yet ready to see the teacher in the classroom firing at little Johnny with live ammunition.

JOAN: But one frequently hears on the media – if one happens to go to America – of injuries and deaths caused by "plastic rounds".

SCROTUM: Don't "happen" to go to America. You won't hear a thing.

JOAN: But what do you tell the parent of a dead child?

SCROTUM: Exactly what I'm telling you now. The EIS is conducting a full enquiry into the matter. You will receive their report in due course.

JOAN: But —

SCROTUM: You see, people have to learn to stand on their own two feet. Even the criminal; that's why I've proposed that long-term prisoners be given the freedom to purchase their own cells.

JOAN: But —

SCROTUM: Yes, even the unemployed. That's why I've proposed that the long-term unemployed be given jobs as grouse-beaters on the Falkland Islands.

JOAN: But the Falklands are as full of unexploded mines as a Scottish dumpling's full of raisins!

SCROTUM: Quite. It's called "rolling back the creeping linoleum of welfarism". And it's got to begin at birth — for that's where the rot sets in. Do you realise that most babies in this country, shortly after delivery, have a fount of warm, comforting goodness stuffed into their mouths — whether they actually want it or not? What sort of a foundation is that for a nation's attitudes!

JOAN: You mean breastfeeding?

SCROTUM: No wonder the first little difficulty these people meet with, the cry goes up, "Doctor, give me a pill", or, "Council, give me a house", or "Taxpayer, give me a feather-bedded life of social-security idleness."

JOAN: Do you wish to abolish breastfeeding?

SCROTUM: No of course I don't want to abolish breastfeeding. I have far too much respect for the fair sex. All I ask is that a child on its delivery should first have the opportunity to be met by a suitably armed and uniformed officer of the state, who could welcome it into the world with a volley of rifle-shots over its head. *Then*, my dear, you could breastfeed the squashed-prune-faced little brat for as long as you wished. Because that child would have learned one lesson it will take through its whole life to the grave.

(*Scrotum on his feet, stiff-backed. He concludes slowly and with great emphasis*) All caring takes place under the Rule of Law!

(*Music. Scrotum sings*)

> God save the Queen
> and the Duke of Edinburgh
> Princess Diana and
> the Prince of Wales
>
> Jimmy Young and
> the Wimbledon Finals
> Any Answers and
> The Horse of the Year
>
> sonata form and
> private education and
> public spending cuts and
> lower taxes
>
> higher rents and
> lower rates and
> no immigration and
> send them all home
>
> the 8 o'clock walk
> and the House of Lords
> and the Master of the Rolls
> and of course Black Rod
>
> Norman Tebbitt
> Peter Manuel
> Sidney Weighell
> and Songs of Praise

the IMF and
the Nato Alliance
the rule of law and
Who Dares Wins!

JOAN: You said recently Mister Scrotum that conscription should be re-introduced. How would you convince the youth of today that this is a proper measure?

SCROTUM: (*sings*)

Fighting really makes
a man of one;
'speshly if
you're unemployed.

Driving tanks is
really super fun;
armour-plated
with sang-froid —

JOAN: But wouldn't these young men be sent to Ulster?

SCROTUM: Of course. Why shouldn't they be? Isn't it Earth's finest training-camp for counter-insurgency activity? You know we in Britain are really so fortunate to have this facility on our own doorsteps. Not like the Americans — they have to go all over the world!

(*sings*)

Join the Army
see ould Ireland
through the night-sight
of a gun;

searching houses
searching shoppers
searching dustbins
— lots o' fun!

REPORTS FROM THE PRESENT

There's the UDR,
there's the RUC
and down Falls Road
— there's a nice cup o' tea!

Ireland, och . . .
Ye canny whack it;
in yer saracen tank
an yer bullet-proof jacket!

On Knowing the Difference between Prejudice, Discrimination and Oppression

This "oppressed person" on £12,000 per year
has composed an article about "macho workerism"
in those analysing today's political situation
in terms of class and economic power.

The machine on which the article has been composed
was itself composed by workers in Taiwan.

These workers were male and female.
Most were heterosexual, some not.
The men got paid more than the women.

The best paid could earn £12,000 in eight years.

Mr Chesty Burns the
Fried Bread

It was a lovely sunny morning in Glasgow, and Mr Chesty was hanging face down over the side of his bed.

That nasty old night phlegm was draining to the top of his lungs.

Poor Mr Chesty!

Cough, cough, cough! At last "The First of the Day" arrived, and Mr Chesty wrapped it in a nice fresh Kleenex.

Mr Chesty peeped.

It was a Mr Happy. "Glasgow's Miles Better!" chirped the little fellow.

Mr Chesty found he could cough up Mr Happys whenever he wanted. And every time Mr Chesty coughed up a Mr Happy, he wrapped it in a nice fresh Kleenex, and put it in the floral bin beside the gas fire.

Soon the floral bin beside the gas fire was full of Mr Happys. "Glasgow's miles better! Glasgow's miles better!" sang the floral bin.

Mr Chesty sat listening to the floral bin. It was just like the Glasgow Orpheus Choir.

"Can you sing 'The Garden Where the Praties Grow?' " asked Mr Chesty. But the floral bin did not know the words.

So Mr Chesty went to make his breakfast.

Mr Chesty put his morning slice of bread in the frying pan, with his morning slice of Lorne. Then he spotted something outside in the garden.

It was a giant inhaler! Mr Chesty went outside to investigate.

The inhaler was almost as big as Mr Chesty himself. Mr Chesty read the label:

CHESTY'S MAGIC INHALER
EXPIR MAR 1995
TWO PUFFS ANYWHERE IN GLASGOW
BEFORE OR AFTER MEALS
STATE DESTINATION CLEARLY

Mr Chesty sat down on the magic inhaler. He pressed the top of the canister twice, and held on tight. "The Burrell Collection!" stated Mr Chesty, clearly.

"Puff! Puff" went the magic inhaler — and rose into the air!

It was the most wonderful day of Mr Chesty's life. He saw all the Glasgow museums. He saw all the galleries. He saw all the parks. He saw the Cathedral. He saw Provand's Lordship.

He had lunch with the Lord Provost at the City Chambers. He heard a symphony concert by the Scottish National Orchestra. He joined in all the coughing between the movements!

But of all the wonderful places that Mr Chesty visited that day, his favourite was the Burrell Collection in Pollok Park.

Do you know who Sir William Burrell was? Can you guess why Mr Chesty felt so proud?

Sir William Burrell was one of Glasgow's most generous and patriotic sons, who had helped his country by selling it ships during the First World War.

Then he had encouraged local business, by spending all the money in Big Peter's cash-and-carry in Maryhill.

One of your no-nonsense Glasgow men, Sir William had liked nothing fancier on his floors than a half-inch of reasonably dry sawdust. So he had hung all Big Peter's carpets and rugs on his walls.

"Sir William was one of us," mused Mr Chesty proudly.

That day was the most marvellous day that the whole city of Glasgow ever saw or heard. For as Mr Chesty flew back and forth over the city on his magic inhaler, the most marvellous thing began to happen.

In all the Mr Happy clinics, people gathered at the windows, waving and tapping on the window-panes with their little inhalers. "Rat-a-tat tat! Rat-a-tat tat!" The sound gathered in unison all over the city. "Rat-a-tat tat! Rat-a-tat tat!"

It was Morse Code. "Glasgow's miles better! Glasgow's miles better!" tapped the happy inhalers.

At last Mr Chesty felt it was time to go home. "Home!" he stated clearly, to the magic inhaler, pressing the top of the canister twice. But nothing happened. "Home, magic inhaler!" said Mr Chesty a little louder.

But all the metered doses had been used up, and the magic inhaler wasn't magic anymore. So Mr Chesty would have to walk.

As Mr Chesty walked home, it was late, it was dark, and it began to rain. It rained so hard, it was like walking through a sea of boiling gobstoppers.

"I'd forgotten tomorrow was Fair Friday!" sighed Mr Chesty.

But that wasn't all that Mr Chesty had forgotten. For when he arrived home, he found that his slice of fried bread had been burnt to a frazzle. And the slice of Lorne was like a wee black postage stamp!

"I'll try to scrape that in the morning," yawned Mr Chesty, and went to his bed.

As Mr Chesty climbed into his bed, he coughed up "The Last of the Day". Mr Chesty wrapped it in a nice fresh Kleenex, and slipped it under his pillow.

"Is it fuck!" snapped the little fellow. "Is it fuck!" It was Mr Pneumonia!! But Mr Chesty didn't hear Mr Pneumonia's nasty bad language. For Mr Chesty was fast asleep.

It was Mr Chesty's lucky night. Already he was dreaming his favourite dream.

In Mr Chesty's favourite dream, he won a magnificent sports trophy. Can you guess what it was called?

THE CAPSTAN FULL-STRENGTH BLOW FOOTBALL SILVER QUAICH

Happy Mr Chesty!

Glasgow's miles better!

The First Nicaraguan Archbishop
of Canterbury

WULLIE: I see McGahey's on his knees to the Archbishop of Canterbury again.

ALEX: Thatcher'll be furious. Still, she just has to act as if she doesny care. She knows Runcie's got too tight a grip on the National Union of Mineworkers.

WULLIE: I don't see what all this religion's got to do with trade unionism. You go to a Scottish branch meeting these days and they're signing agreements with pens shaped like John Knox. And coachloads of flying priests everywhere. And Len Murray speaking in the tongues!

ALEX: You're just blinkered Wullie. You think established religion has always been the enemy of working people. Not true. Look at Archbishop Runcie's tour of South America.

WULLIE: Eh?

ALEX: Forgotten already have you. Forgotten how he refused to shake the hand of a single South American dictator? Forgotten the tongue-lashing he gave Pinochet?

WULLIE: (*doubtfully*) Oh aye . . .

ALEX: Forgotten how his speeches and sermons all over South America were on the evils of poverty and oppression? On the killing of thousands of trade unionists and their families by soldiers and state murder-gangs? How the clergy ought to involve itself more fully on the side of the oppressed?

181

WULLIE: (*even more doubtfully*) Oh aye . . .

ALEX: Look at that service in Nicaragua. Who would have thought that one day we'd see the head of a Christian community stand in a Nicaraguan pulpit, openly denouncing the dirty work of the USA. The courage and vision of the man!

WULLIE: I must have missed that . . .

ALEX: All he lacks is charisma. That's his only trouble. He's all principles. No charisma.

WULLIE: Principles ma rump! The bloodshed of Capitalism he'll always criticise, but of Communism – never. Of American Imperialism, yes – but of Russian, never. Look at when he went to Poland.

ALEX: Archbishop Runcie?

WULLIE: Yes. There was no nudge-nudge wink-wink criticism of the government *there*, was there? Oh no – but plenty of "key words in the speeches" having a go at trade unions!

ALEX: Yes but –

WULLIE: I've no respect for a man who tours South America criticising the governments, then goes to Poland and criticises the people!

ALEX: But Wullie, Archbishop Runcie was *born* in Nicaragua, you realise that, don't you?

WULLIE: The fact that he's the first Nicaraguan Archbishop of Canterbury makes no difference!

ALEX: Oh that's not true Wullie. It's a great achievement being the first Nicaraguan Archbishop of Canterbury. And he's doing a wonderful job with the National Union of Mineworkers.

Thought for the Day

with
The Reverend Jimmy Gelmayel
of
The Maronite Christian Church,
Lebanon

Good Evening.

You know, I bet you've all met the chap who'll tell you that were Christ alive today he would be a member of the Campaign for Nuclear Disarmament.

That he would be a Pacifist.

Perhaps, even, that he would walk the streets unarmed.

It's a nice thought, isn't it. The real world seems so much harsher.

I still remember the shock I got that day my grandmother first told me that Christ could have avoided the crucifixion, if only God could have cut off American aid to Herod. But it was written in the Book of Life that he should die for our sins.

Your sins. And mine.

So even as Christ carried his cross to Golgotha, the missiles, the tanks, the aircraft, the dollars – yes, even those phosphorous shells that burn inside the flesh and can't be extinguished – all these were pouring into Jerusalem from America.

It seems so cruel, doesn't it.

The man of peace, surrounded by such weapons of war.

But History's a funny thing.

I was on my rounds in Beirut the other day when a little Palestinian boy approached me in the street.

"Mister," he said, "are you a Christian?"

"Of course," I answered.

"You Christians are worse than the Israelis," he said. "At least when the Israelis massacre us, they bury the bodies in mass graves. They bulldoze the houses, and make the ground flat and clean for the western reporters. But when you Christians massacre us, you leave the bodies to stink in the sun."

"Strong words," some of you might say. "Typical terrorist talk," I can hear others thinking; and no doubt, had that wee laddie been allowed to grow up, a terrorist is what he would have grown to be.

But as I resumed my walk that morning, I found myself deep in thought. I thought about my own childhood; and about the need to keep our own children safe.

Now I don't know if you know it, but there are folk who would like to see religious education abolished in the schools.

Atheists.

Marxists.

Folk who have let their faith go cold.

"If you want religious education," these people say, "give them it at home."

Now all I would want to say is this.

Here in Lebanon, there has been a wonderful co-operation between Jew and Christian, and the world has borne witness to what this can achieve. But I'm going to say something now that will surprise you.

Surely this co-operation between Christian and Jew need not be confined to Lebanon?

Why not in Scotland? Why not in the schools?

It may seem a bit far-fetched.

But it's a thought.

Will you say a wee prayer with me?

186

THOUGHT FOR THE DAY

Dear Father in Heaven, we thank Thee for the fruits of that wonderful co-operation between Jew and Christian in Lebanon, and we ask Thee in Thy bounty to bestow on Thy Jewish and Christian children on earth that same mercy which together they have shown unto others.
Through Christ Our Lord.
Amen.

Good Evening. And if you're not a Palestinian, God bless you.

How I Became a
Sound Poet

Sometime in the early sixties, I heard on the radio Bob Cobbing's sound-poem, "Are Your Children Safe in the Sea". As I remember it from that listening, it was like a set of performance variations, each rendering of the sentence having a very different inflexion, and different pace. It was very menacing, very daemonic – and very funny. It was also, according to Jack de Manio who introduced it on his morning radio magazine programme, a Load of Rubbish. I thought it was great though. I also thought that another sound-poem I heard around this time, Brion Gysin's "I Am That I Am", was great too. At any rate I fell out of bed beating time to it. This was a response usually reserved for Berlioz and the last movement of Bruckner symphonies.

Round about 1968, at the suggestion of Tom McGrath, I decided to pursue these matters myself. Using a small cassette, I put together a performance piece which I called "The Horn of the Hunter". For the first part of this, I recorded the slow movement of Scriabin's First Symphony, accompanied by a friend's simulation of a protracted orgasm. While she was thus simulating, I recorded various interjections mainly concerned with the words "Rosaleen" and "shite". The ensuing sections consisted of extracts from a reported conversation between a schizophrenic patient and a psychiatrist ("Do you know how you got here?" "No," – very Beckettish) and some statistics to do with suicides in Britain, which I had obtained from a Pelican. At some point in the performance I sang "Kathleen Mavourneen", which included the line "The horn of the hunter

191

is heard on the hill." A member of the audience was primed to shout, from the back of the hall, "Is there something wrong with the narrator's hypothalamus?"

Some years after this, I was introduced to Bob Cobbing himself. The outcome was an invitation to appear in one of Bob's annual sound-poetry festivals, in London in May 1975. In trusting me to come up with something for his festival, Bob was in a way commissioning me and throwing me in at the deep end. I prepared two works – one called "My Name is Tom", the other "Ach Caledonia". Using a two-track stereo machine, in the first piece I broke down the sentence "My name is Tom" into vowels, phonemes, and permed variations on the original structure of the sentence. Using my voice in recording a tape, I worked my way systematically through a range of emotions: in a way, the more I shattered the sentence, the more assertive and confident the emotions I gave to the bits. So these two components were at odds with each other. The two separate tracks (recorded in parallel mono) I tried to make repeatedly in conflict with each other too, in terms of separately fluctuating volume, and in their separately vying for the listener's attention between differing deliberately tantalising bits. As a third "channel" I wrote a series of quotations for the narrator – i.e. myself – to say, shout, and sing. "Kathleen Mavourneen" made her comeback, and there were sections from *Paradise Lost* and *Biggles Flies North*. A conversation between Biggles and Ginger crumbled into a dialogue about the metaphysical basis of the naming process, transposed from Sapir's *Culture, Language, and Personality*. Finally, as a fourth "silent" channel, I wrote out a series of placards to be held up in rotation during the performance, partly creating a rhythm of their own. The placards began by making phonetic representations of the sentence "My name is Tom" broken up – MM . . . AYE . . . NN . . . AI . . . etc. – but moved into words that led to the conflict of cultures partly at the heart of the thing, JEAN PAUL SETT'ERDAY SANNY SARTRE. The whole work I tried to keep together bearing in mind Nielsen's instruction to the drummer in the first movement of his Fifth Symphony: to improvise as if to drown the progress of the orchestra. The "as if" was the heart of the matter.

The "Ach Caledonia" piece used basically the same format of parallel mono tape tracks, narrator, and placards. The basic conflict here (analysing it after the event) could roughly be called that between a dependent and an independent – or counter-dependent – psychological attitude. On the tapes there were lengthy variations (mostly in terms of bitterness) on ways to pronounce "Ach"; both narrator and tape sometimes sought increasingly whining ways of saying "Ma mammy's doon it the laundry," and there was an awful leave-me-alone voice that went on and on about this restaurant where you could get a whole pot of tea, not a cup, and tatties and steak pie and you know how in some places the peas are always cold well here they're always just straight from the pot and the plate is that hot you can hardly touch it and so on and so on. The first main quote declaimed by the narrator in the performance was the eight lines from Scott's "The Lady of the Lake" beginning "O Caledonia, stern and wild/ Meet nurse for a poetic child!" and two quotes from Grotowski on the theatre, one of which stated that Artaud had realised that with the demise of a common faith there could only be conflict between performer and audience. This was spoken in a smug, prissy wee voice. Most of the narrator's declamation in "Ach Caledonia" though (there was no singing) was from a collage I'd previously written called "The Faith of Our Fathers, or God Save the Quing". Loosely derived from a book about patriarchy (I think) I'd read before, called *Society Without the Father*, the collage had consisted of a series of more or less elliptical references to the psychology of slow/quick male/female characteristics of Glasgow speech, and how "a computer could have predicted R. D. Laing fifty years ago". There was a deal about the Catholic–Protestant Celtic–Rangers business seen in terms of dependent–counterdependent symbols and characteristics, mostly abbreviated to placard form. A placard held aloft in the middle of the work showed an aerial plan of a football stadium with the crowds in position for a Celtic–Rangers football match. The placard was captioned OEDIPUS SCREWING HIS MOTHER AT BOTH ENDS. Perhaps because of the amount of logical stuff the narrator had to spout out, the placards used were mostly in fact deliberately illogical in their sequential message, like the opening TICKLY MINCE . . . A BLUE SKY . . . A DEAF EGG . . . OVER. As in "My Name is Tom", the placards in sequence held aloft by the narrator at the beginning of the work, were held aloft in the same sequence at the end.

The two sound-poems, both lasting just under ten minutes, seemed to go down quite well with the audience in London. In fact in some ways they evoked the best response at a performance I've ever received, as a Canadian in the audience presented me as I left with a full half-bottle of Canadian whiskey, and a cassette on which he asked me to record my experiences as I drank it. His address was written on the side of the cassette, he told me. Unfortunately he must have drunk a deal of Canadian whiskey himself before he made the gesture, as his name and address proved later to be totally illegible.

After the London festival I was regularly invited to sound-poetry events in different places, and at these I became familiar with the work of leading European and American performers. With Joan Hughson I organised the international festivals "Sound and Syntax" in 1978, and "Poetsound 84" last year. Both were held in the Third Eye Centre, though the more recent festival was not restricted to sound-poetry. Among the sound poets who did come to either or both Glasgow festivals were Ernst Jandl and Gerhard Rühm from Austria, Jackson MacLow and Jerome Rothenberg from America, Henri Chopin and Bernard Hiedsieck from France, Lily Greenham from Denmark, Franz Mon from Germany, Katalin Ladik from Yugoslavia, bp Nichol from Canada. As to what the definition of "sound-poetry" is, I've never heard a satisfactory definition yet, and it's not a question that interests me. The poets I've listed all have very different styles, some working with tape-recorders, some not. My main reason for wanting them to be heard in Scotland was because they all had struck me as a hundred per cent authentic artists, whose means of expression was obviously essential to them, an essential part of themselves as individuals. Not every person wanting to be thought of as a sound poet has struck me that way. Bad art is one thing, bad conceptual art can be bloody awful. It usually has to be reached through extensive suburbs of philosophical jargon, I find.

Regarding the development of my own work with tapes since 1975, it's been confined basically to a series of five-minute two-track settings of pieces of literature – a bit from Kierkegaard's *Either/Or*, a stanza from Shelley's "The Revolt of Islam", some verses from the Book of Job. My last completed piece was a setting of the sonnet "Shall I compare thee to a summer's day", which I built up to 164 overlapping voices, arranged in a fairly simple symmetrical shape, framed by the refrain "Nor shall Death brag thou wand'rest in his shade". But I haven't been doing much work of this kind at all recently. It's partly because the soundproofing in my house has been very poor since the whole tenement was "renovated" a couple of years ago. Eggboxes on the walls of the little room I record in just aren't enough. So I can only do quiet things: my last attempted one, to be called "Report of a Literary Conversation in which the Author Recently Took Part", consisted solely of elaborate variations on the phrase "niggle niggle"; but not being able unselfconsciously to relax and let my voice go as loud as I liked is probably why the thing didn't really work out to my satisfaction.

But another reason I've stopped is because I found the process itself of making sound-poems very psychologically unsettling. It's bad enough having to do draft upon draft – as I do – when writing, but having to do this with a tape recorder when you've headphones on, produces some fairly weird states of mind. I got to the point where when people were talking to me, I would instinctively be trying to assess what tracks they were on – i.e. 1 and 3, or 2 and 4. It's unsettling to have to remind yourself that the recording machine you are now using is called your brain, that this is reality, and there is no rewind button. Also I found, whenever I was working hard at my tape recorder for any length of time, that this Old Testament God voice always came along. He was very fingerwaggy and had a severe opinion of life in general, and mine in particular. I found him very handy for my setting of the Book of Job, but after that I got tired of him, and decided to let him remain encased in my machine. If he wants out for a walk, he must now confine himself to my dreams. Long live repression!

Of Whigling Provosts

[impending General Election 1987]

I don't believe a word of them. I don't believe Kinnock would remove nuclear missiles or bases. The so-called Hard Left is keeping its mouth shut because the non-nuclear card is the only Left card that Kinnock has. And it's not even Left, it's Liberal. But the anti-nuclear Liberals are keeping their mouths shut because of Owen and the Alliance.

You go for a day out to Dunoon and there's one of the submarines heading out to sea just when you're having a bit of relaxation, letting your mind go blank. You go for a holiday in Crete and when you're learning the constellations at night with your son you begin to notice all the satellites nightly crossing the sky. The only English station you can pick up is the American base, Radio Heraklion. They're everywhere.

What is a conventional weapon, that's what I'd like to know. Is it one of those phosphorous ones that burn under the skin? Is an Exocet conventional? When laser weapons are developed, will these be called conventional or not? If they're conventional, does that mean a Labour government could stock up with billions of pounds' worth?

*

John Henderson, my jo, John,
   I think the step was wrang
That led ye 'mang the Chartist crood
   Or sic a graceless gang;

For they, the fules, were serious,
   An' onward meant to go,
An' ye ken it wisna sae wi' you,
   John Henderson, my Jo.

John Henderson, my jo, John,
   Ye turned in time tae see
That neither cash nor Provostships
   The Chartists had tae gie;
You're now a Whigling Provost, John,
   But mair a Whig you'll grow,
An' you'll maybe be our member yet,
   John Henderson, my jo.

John Henderson, my jo, John,
   I'm proud indeed tae tell,
That aye whate'er the public did,
   Ye minded weel yoursel';
Your nest you've snugly feathered, John,
   In spite o' frien' or foe,
An' that was a' ye bargain'd for
   John Henderson, my jo.

               (Edward Polin, 1841)

*

A sceptical American friend has written you a derogatory letter about the Lord Chancellor: it describes him as "slumped on his woolly sack like five stone of Golden Wonders". Write an informal letter to your friend correcting his misunderstandings. Describe the triple doff-hatting significance of the inauguration of bishops.

A recently appointed Knight of the Garter has besought your permission "to wear it round my middle leg". Draft a proclamation allowing him to do so at specific state ceremonial occasions. Itemise those at which this would be held as not in keeping with the dignity of office.

Estimate how many bicycles would be required to transport those members of parliament who are council-house tenants. Write an essay showing why this exemplifies the health of our democracy.

If a Party Leader smiles forty-three times in one hour, calculate how many pence per smile over forty hours would earn him a Youth Training Scheme wage.

*

What's a conventional weapon, that's what I'd like to know. Is parliament a closed value-system that renders honest dialogue impossible? Does every dominant aspect of British culture have to present such when analysed? Do you think, ach well, I'll vote if the local candidate's really Left, if not forget it?

the freedom of choice

capitalism.

welfare capitalism.
capitalism with a bit more welfare than the last one.

nationalistic capitalism.
capitalism that really cares about industrial pollution.
vegetarian capitalism.

eccentric capitalism – capitalism in funny hats and rosettes.

*

what country were you born in –
does your government need to borrow capital?
how do the repayments affect you? How much interest per
   year?

do you get hungry? do you have a decent place to stay?

*

You go for a day out to Dunoon and there's one of the submarines heading out to sea just when you're having a bit of relaxation, letting your mind go blank. You go for a holiday in Crete and when you're learning the constellations at night with your son you begin to notice all the satellites nightly crossing the sky. The only English station you can pick up is the American base, Radio Heraklion. They're everywhere.

Sourscenes from Scottish
Literary Life

1.

o am no a
ehm
am noa ehm

puritan like
naw
nay wey

jist
ahm eh
am

that eh
serious
its

ma art
aye
fuck me am

aye

thats it

2.

one of those writers always suspicious of laughter
at the heart of whose work is a concept of masculinity

sifting for sellouts every chuckle of an audience
mean hombres don't look for approval know what I mean

hung up on reverence: reverence for the cowboy
lolling home from the frontier, pioneer

swashbuckling shucks, washbucklin sucks
nickers off ready when I come home

3.

Your work has been declared relevant
by the vanguardist literary publication
of a southern foreign capital.

Receive two invitations to launches:
but be warned —

Some of your friends are now enemies.

4.

This one is ambitious.
Come: let us spend a year
inside his head!

5.

the mainstream of world literature
has this moment been re-routed

to arrive at the Collected Works
of yonder two drunks:

no wonder they look happy!

6.

the haemorrhoidal pot-bellied visiting dialect poet
silently eases a blood-drenched fart

into the already semiotically overladen immediate ambience
of the incessantly talking lecturer on socio-psycho-linguistics

7.
the excited blurb

". . . larger than life,
it is smaller than the Cosmos only by
that volume which you now hold in your hand.
This book is all that it is not!"

After the nuclear obliteration of Scotland, a fragment of a long poem is found in a lead coffin

Of course as Stalin clearly demonstrated in *Marxism and Problems of Linguistics*:

> . . . the significance of the so-called gesture language, in view of its extreme poverty and limitations, is negligible. Properly speaking, this is not a language, and not even a linguistic substitute that could in one way or another replace spoken language, but an auxiliary means of extremely limited possibilities to which man sometimes resorts to emphasise this or that point in his speech. Gesture language and spoken language are just as incomparable as are the primitive wooden hoe and the modern caterpillar tractor with its five-furrow plough or tractor row drill.

This in incontrovertible contradistinction to the terracing rice-pudding-brain whose idea of Scottish Literature consists of readings from Charlie Tully's *Passed to You*:

> If I had a pound for every time I've sent a corner kick swinging into the goalmouth at practice, I'd be a millionaire. When I'm at outside-left, I place the ball in the arc, take a step back and send it over with my right foot. I reverse the procedure if I'm on the right. This is the only proper way to take a flag kick – that is, if you want to put the ball into the danger zone. The ball takes a curve and swings in on goal making it awkward for a goal-keeper to cover it all the way.

A Handy Form for Artists
for use in connection with
the City of Culture

Date as postmark

Dear

Thank you for your *invitation*/ commission** for me to *participate*/
contribute*/ display*/ write an article*/ write a play*/ write a poem*/
sing*/ discuss*/ act*/ conduct*/ read from my work*/*
play the   *, †

at   Glasgow
on   the   of   1990.

I note that this   *is being wholly or partly sponsored from
funds allocated for*/ uses advertising material that mentions*/ is
being described as part of*/ does not effectively dissociate itself
from*/*
†
the so-called "City of Culture" programme of events.

I regret that I cannot accept your *invitation*/ commission*/*
because

it is a matter of conscience too tedious to explain/ City Culture
yes City of a Culture yes City of Culture no*/ the slogan is a nasty
piece of advertising language meaning: a) places and people are
worth something as to whether or not they can be described as "of
Culture" b) that desirable thing-to-be-owned, Culture, is now
owned by Glasgow c) City of Culture = Person of Culture =
Someone who does not enter the drawing room with cheese on
their whiskers*/ it is as much an insult to Beethoven and Rem-
brandt as it is to so-called "community art" and to any citizen past
or present*/ any participating artist, work of art, or event will appear*

213

within the programme as an exemplification of this right-wing tourist slogan*/ critical or "left-wing" works within the programme will function as "the antibodies necessary to keep the body politic healthy" — which it most certainly isn't*/ come-on-in the labour's cheap and the entertainment's good*/ come-on-in Razor King has been buried with his bunnit*/ †

and because I am fed up with

the relentless use of the word "celebration" in connection with Glasgow by mediapersons*/ my children getting crap food at school because of dinnerschool cutbacks*/ with public service workers being laid off, or their wages driven down "so that we can hold on to the tender"*/ with my health service being destroyed what about people with things like emphysema, it's not all smoking this city is cold and damp*/ with it being a crime to be under 25*/ with them agreeing to sell the council houses*/ with poor and unemployed people being systematically harassed and deprived of benefits, within this city*/ with the unemployment figures, and all the other statistics, everybody knows they're shite, when am I going to turn on my radio or television and hear honest language*/ with the land around Glasgow practically crackling with radioactivity you soon won't even be able to go to Saltcoats for a paddle*/ why do the lamb chops in the butchers glow in the dark*/ why don't they put turnstiles on the housing schemes and make them Deprived Heritage Museums*/ with all this Mr Even Happier nonsense*/
†

Yours sincerely

(citizen of Glasgow)*

* delete if inapplicable   † insert other if necessary

Ablative Absolute

having been seized with the dry boke
at the state opening of parliament

black rod delicately applied
the instrument of his nomenclature

to the back of his throat

The Moderate Member's
Monologue

Christ. Thank fuck I'm an MP.

I mean naw, really. Majn been poor, eh. Majn been really poor. Majn no huvn a job or sumthin. Ur been wan a they YTS people. Christ Almighty. Fuck me. Majn been under 25 eh. Fuckin hell. Aw jesus. Majn been really poor an a wummin ur sumhm, an yir man's left yi. (*shakes his head*)

Majn livn ina council house. Christ.

Ahv nuthn against council houses minji. Loat a ma constituents live in thim. Aye. A wuz broat up in a council house. Thir aw right council houses. Yi ever seen a council house?

Pity ma da dyin. Yi lose touch wi yir roots.

Ma memories fuckt as well. Sometimes a wish everybody wiz jist cawd thi same name. Like the men aw cawd Harry an thi wummin aw cawd Reena. Hello Harry. Hello Reena. It's been a long time Reena. How's the leg Harry. Yi stull wurkn n Barr N Strouds.

No that a ivir wurkt n Barr N Strouds.

Naw. That law digree wuz the best thing a done. That n joinin the party. Yil get naywhere unless yir a lawyer that's whut they tellt mi. Ur a lecturer.

Christ a hate socialists. A hate left-wing people. A really dae. They really get on ma tits. Fuckin branch is riddled wi thim.

Neil'll soart thaim oot though. Already huz. Aye. "Spread democracy". Fuck yiz. Get thi fuckin block votes oan thim. Boomp.

Didyi see thi conference. Goodyin this year wintit. Really

fuckt thim this time, gave thim a right good doin. Thi constituencies a mean.

That wuzza good idea that scattern thi constituencies through the hall. Mine they aw used tay sit thigithir, it lookt bad that. This big forest a hawns doon wan side a thi hall ivri time some left-wing rubbish wuz proposed. Took a cuppla big block votes tay wipe thim aw oot. Lookt bad nthi telly aye. Am aw fur this new image stuff.

Aye. A hate socialists. We wur supposed tay be getn a few new wans this time in the new MPs. Aye. The doomsday scenario. Very revolutionary eh. Christ. Donald sorted thaim oot quick enough. He's really good at his joab. He'd make a great minister. Ye'll no hear a cheep fray thaim.

Ah thoat wid a hud tay dae a few marches thoa. Dae the Blythswood Square tay Glasgow Green walk again. Cuppla puddens up front tryin tay look determined. That STUC guy. What's his name. Christ a canny remembir his fuckin name. He's good though. Wanny uz. Ah we'll need ti day sumhm aboot thi poll tax. Stoap folk breakn thi law.

Ah think this art caper's a good idea. Getn aw thi writers in init. Yeh a mean. Thirza few a thim aboot. It's better that. A night oot, a lot a gags aboot thi ugly face a Thatcherism an that. Keeps us united. A mean that's whut's needed thi noo above anythin else. Unity. Aye. Ahm aw for that. A mean fur Christ sake who wahnts satire that makes yi feel uncomfortable. No me.

Ach though a don't really care. A mean the left-wing's that fuckt it doesny really matter anyway. Aw gin aboot wi their glazed eyes. Fuckin mass hypnagogic state. Whair um a. This izny happnin. Great eh.

Aye. Get the writers gawn. A saysti a cuppla thim, come on, time you cunts put yir shoulder tay the wheel. Join the team. No much money in it but. But we'll get yi a few gigs. The clubs, demos. Pahrty rallies. Ahll put you in touch wi a few guys get yi a wee cabaret tour. How does that grab yi. Maybe a wee tour afore the local elections, few late night spots. Cheap bevvy, that should wind yous up. Courss you writers, youll be on yir hole eftir aw thi readins. Lucky bastards.

Naw ahm a family man but. Ma daughter. God ma daughter. Fyi think a hate thi Left yi should hear her on the Tories. She's a teacher. Christ a widny be Michael Forsyth if she got a hawdy im. Coorss she blames us but. "If you lot hudny put the pressure on Pollok we'd a won wir strike." That's what she tells mi. "Coz a you an thi sell-out Communists ahv got an hours unpaid overtime tay dae ivry week. Is that whut you call a victory?"

Lissn madam, a says. Lissn Madam. Dae yi think we'd go inty an election backin a national strike? Dae yi think we drappt thi fuckin miners in thi shite jist tay bail yous out?" Coorss that's aw wahter aff a duck's back. (*imitates her*) "The Coal Board's got nothin on Strathclyde Region when it comes tay closures. Whut wans will we shut? (*rubs his hands*) Jist fight among yirsell fur thirty days!" Great wan fur jokes ma daughter. (*imitates her*) "How does the Labour Party rose no huv any pricks on it. Mawn. How does thi Labour Party rose no huv any pricks on it. Coz Mr Kinnock didny chair the selection committee." "I'd like a penny for every time Neil Kinnock's mentioned the word class. Why would you like a penny for every time Neil Kinnock's mentioned the word class? Because then if I'd only nine more pence I could buy a packet of polo mints."

Ach well. We got thi last laugh anyway. That election campaign shut the left up. No that they'd opened their mooths fur a few months afore it but. Anyway. Aye. Yiv goat tay be realistic. If yi canny kerry Fleet Street an the Nine a Cloak News thirz nay hope a yir marginals. No that ahm in a marginal. Ah reckn ahv got thurty years yet. Stull maybe a should go at seventy.

A suppose thirz better jobs though. Look at wee Paul. Imagine bein Director a Council Houses fur Glasgow an yi get a job wi thi firm thats buyin thim aw up. Good onyi Mister Maignanni! (*spreads his arms, smiles broadly*) It's aw legal as well, they canny even stick im in the jail. An jist wait tay thi schools ur sellt aff – think a thi real estate. As Neil would say (*gives thumbs-up sign*) – Smashing!

Naw it's got to be realistic now. Ahm all for this lissnin exercise. Two years tay we finally tell thi Left officially at last tay go an take a runnin fuck tay itsell. That unilateral shite's out the window for starters. No that we'd ever a done it anyway but sayn we wid was the price a keepn the so-called hard left quiet aboot everythin else in their utopia. Naw there's times yi huv tay offer yir enemies a carrot. But they times are past, thank fuck. We're no gawny waste aw that money we'll huv spent on Trident by the time we're elected. Naw that'll be a fait accompli an cunts like Livingstone'll jist huv tay swally that ur leave. Yi don't buy a guard dug then take it back tay the shoap.

A think Trident could be a vote-catcher though, especially if we offer the workers shares in it. Why not? A mean it's thi ordnary voter yi wahnt tay reach no thi activists. An let's face it thi ordnary voters got a heed fuhll a *Sun* newspapers.

Talkn aboot thaht ahd better be away. Ahm tryn tay get this piece done fur the papers. An auld ex-communist mate said he'd pit in a word for me in the *Sun*. Aye. Noo, there's the kinna socialist a really like. (*imitates*) "Yi know, the most sensible socialist in the entire history of socialism, has been Jesus Christ. Jist imagine. That man was God. He could have pulled out the whole Roman army at one snap of his fingers. If he'd wanted he could have had every worker in the whole Roman Empire down tools and walk off the job. But what did he say? 'Render unto Caesar the things that are Caesar's, and to God the things that are God's.' That's what he said. And the next time I hear a so-called socialist say that no-strike agreements are betraying the working class, I'll say, 'What about Mark Chapter Twelve Verse Seventeen?' "

(*winks*) Aye. Wirra broad church. (*angrily*) But no *that* broad.

from
The Front-of-the-Mouth
Oral Activity Member

That's what I loved about Glenalmond. The fresh air, the rigour. And the fact one could walk with a straight back, because one knew one's parents were putting their hands in their pockets and handing over hard cash, cash you could bite on or hold up to the light and see the watermark through Her Majesty the Queen. That's what exaggerated-front-of-the-mouth oral activity is all about. Watermarks. If you hold a note up to the light, you ought to be able to see a man looking out at you wearing a crinkly wig. If that man could speak, he would be promising to pay the bearer on demand. Not many people realise he's wearing one of this society's most sacred totems. I sometimes think that the crinkly wig of dead hair has been God's greatest gift to the British people. It is our tablet of stone, set against the gilded calf of trade unionism.

It strikes me as being of the utmost importance that crinkly wigs of dead hair are not available over the counter. That's why I'm bringing in my Crinkly Wig of Dead Hair Retail Restrictions Act. This should confine the sale of crinkly wigs to those who have met on the level and parted on the square. I think I can rely on the whips.

Now I was talking to Black Rod the other day – there's a fine chap if ever there was one – and we were discussing all this boorishness in the House of Commons. "It's not new ye know, Alex," he said. "Not many people realise that one of our greatest statesmen, the Younger Pitt, was so overcome with claret during one debate that he was physically sick behind the Speaker's chair."

"It's a good job he's not living now, Roddie," I replied. "He would have been drummed out of the Labour Party!"

Actually Roddie and I were just returning from tea in the Members' Cafeteria. It had been quite a gathering. There was Baron Fitt of the Divis, Lord Carmichael of Byres Road, and good Old Uncle Jim Callaghan sporting his new garter. He rolled up his trousers and showed us it hanging just above the knee. "I got this for clamming up about MI6 and Lord Gannex," he says proudly. "Her Majesty and Margaret rushed it through in a fortnight. They tried to palm me off with an Order of the Bath but I told them to fuck off. I'm for the Privy Council or else I'm going to demand an enquiry," he says, banging his big *nouveau riche* mitts on the members' cafeteria table.

It was quite embarrassing. My old friend John Carlisle – he's the honourable member for Johannesburg – he turns to me and says, "You know Alex you can put these chaps in the House of Lords and they're *still* not ready for democracy."

John was telling me the other day about this new ad for YTS that Lord Young's come up with. Now there's a chap that knows how to wear ermine. Anyway this ad shows a young girl telling about how she got a job with the Youth Training Scheme and it's just the best thing that's happened to her in her life. The ad begins with her talking on some kind of screen but then the camera backs away to show it's a roll of toilet paper. And while she's still talking away about how she used to hear all these horror stories, all untrue, this hand comes up from the left of the screen and pulls off the perforated piece with her face on it. It's absolutely wonderful photography and of course you're so fascinated you're just totally engrossed while she blethers away. Anyway she's describing how she'd been really lonely and depressed before starting YTS when the camera shows that it's Lord Young holding the torn-off paper with her talking face on it, which he then wipes his arse with before chucking it down the pan.

And the miracle is. You see this crumpled-up face at the bottom of the bowl, still talking, about how she's made wonderful new friends and got a job in the planning department. And then Lord Young pulls the chain.

But that's only the beginning . . .

Pound and MacDiarmid:
From a Seventies Notebook

Pound was every inch a fascist as MacDiarmid was a communist. Both first gained a reputation by writing in what could be considered an archaic style. Both were primarily lyrical, later hortatory and didactic. Both regarded particular knowledge to be gained from particular books as vital to the maintenance of civilisation. MacDiarmid wrote hymns to Lenin. Pound wrote hymns to Mussolini. Both admired strong male leadership. Both "lacked sympathy". Both were inventive flyters, with a talent for venom and with memorable scatalogical attacks on the veneer of the English poetry scene. Both had contempt for the ignorance of the masses. Both attempted synoptic views of history. Both were convinced of their own genius and centrality. Both were pointedly arcane in their references. Both were totally committed, urgent.

MacDiarmid wrote "In Memoriam James Joyce". Pound got Joyce published.

Pound's support for Mussolini did not waver after the invasion of Ethiopia. MacDiarmid rejoined the Communist Party after the Russian suppression of the Hungarian uprising. Both were convinced that they knew what was good for the world, and the world would be greatly improved were the knowledge, to which they had specific access, made general.

Both were like siamese twins, seemingly inevitable in retrospect.

One a communist the other a fascist. But of the two it is the communist who has appealed more to the linguistically conservative, the keep-Scotland-as-Scottish-as-it-once-was, or the look-at-that, never-read-a-book-in-his-life brigade. The inviolability of the Word. A Bible-based, reformation culture. Puritanism. The Protestant ethic and the spirit of capitalism? Through the Word people acquire value. Names and lists. In Catholicism this sacramentalist, ritualistic – Hopkins, Mackay Brown etc. But Muir? So many taboos around MacDiarmid's name. Especially by those who make their living out of teaching Literature, or write poetry influenced by him. One is not allowed to ask five minutes to be a person, in freedom alone in the world to read him. Even to suggest this is to be who do you think you are, to be accused of the most spiteful personal attack, of meanspiritedness, jealousy, philistinism, anti-Scottishness, typical parochial envy of the great, and so on and so forth. The captains of industry and the "Scottish Literature" industry. What are they afraid of. Why do they have to be so vicious in anticipation of less than reverence? Why is the notion of reverence itself consistently so relevant? And the fascist Pound whose prosody is used as a basis in Cardenal's mass poetry workshops in Nicaragua.

Both had personal charm distinct from the cantankerousness of their written opinions.

Pound saw himself as a kind of aristocratic underdog, who could only link with a humanity denied aristocracy by "tribes" who supposedly functioned to maintain this true humanity's underdog position.

MacDiarmid saw himself as an intellectual aristocrat amongst underdogs, whose hope of salvation lay in their consciousness being somehow raised, in Scotland, to the level of his own.

Some day MacDiarmid's work will be allowed to be a person, probably in about fifty years.

20 years later. In response to the centenary, 1992

A relief to open a book of poetry, and to find yourself in the presence of a brain.

Enjoying for some time now the space at least and at last to meet him, read him and enjoy his work alone and in peace. This especially after the collapse of the Soviet Empire, and the prospect that the work might at last genuinely need to be defended.

So much of what used to be objectionable was to do with the corona around his work, full of folk with the most obnoxious anti-art, anti-life attitudes. People with reason not to see poetry as expression from one individual universally to another, but as some kind of "contribution to Modern Scottish Literature": often people who imagined themselves to be guardians, managers and definers of same; MacDiarmid's work absolutely central, a foundation, to the concept they imagined they had not only to defend but to create. Or else they saw themselves as part of the second wave breaking on the shore and so on. It was pathetic, some of it at least.

Hoping that "centenary celebrations" do not spoil the peace of this attained oasis, by releasing a last giant birthday-tide of truly bourgeois reifying and religiose cant.

A Night at the Pictures
After Duhamel

For Sonya

Some time ago my wife Sonya and myself went to the Glasgow Film Theatre, formerly the Cosmo. We went to see a French film called *Jean de Florette*, which had received some good reviews. Unfortunately between our house and the cinema, my wife and myself had a row. I cannot remember what it was about, or any of the details, but as we entered the cinema she delivered a particularly wounding remark, in a quiet voice. I was not going to sit having a night-out as if nothing had happened, but to storm out would have been histrionic. As the film began I therefore found that I was staring at a position on the ceiling somewhere north-west, five to eleven, of the screen itself.

The position of my head was such that a person who did not have a sight of my eyes would have assumed that I was watching the film. I did not want to disturb anyone else in the cinema by making a public issue of my estrangement from the communal event. Gradually I began to "take in" where I was – without moving my position other than the occasional quasi-relaxational shift that would divert potential awareness in others of an unnatural rigidity in one of the group.

The dialogue that filled the theatre seemed a little harsh and loud, as if it needed some adjustment to the volume and the treble. Also the words were in French, which did not help me, as I only understand it at a simple level, spoken slowly. There were long periods without dialogue, the sound of what was perhaps a cow, of people breathing. Feet on floors, utensils, sounds that indicated a scene indoors. Voices evidently shouting from a distance meant that the action had moved once more outside. The most dramatic point was when the cinema was suddenly filled with the sound of a thunderstorm, while a man shouted at the top of his voice, then started weeping. All the while I kept my eyes averted from the screen. A couple of times my wife asked me if I was all right. I replied that I was.

Away from the screen, the quality of light that the screen threw on the walls and ceiling was surprisingly mixed, jumpy, changing all the time; I could see the varied light on the crowns of people near the front, the varying darkness at the small of their backs. Inevitably – I was in an end seat in the balcony – I could see angled shoes at the aisle's edge opposite, the usual light at the carpet shining on a man's sock at the ankle. But it was the silence that really struck me: the silence of the people around me, above all the silence of the building that was not this talking wall at which I couldn't look. The door with its sign EXIT – saying nothing. The building revealed itself as a wall of silence, literally, between the screen and the world. This in the red light that shone faintly on my wife and myself, noticeable in the darker moments, from one of the pinlights above us.

Then it was over, and we were out. I felt I had maybe gone beyond a mark, broken a primitive taboo between friends. But to have called it the breaking of a primitive taboo would maybe have been to load it with a significance it did not deserve. After all, it had just been a huff. When asked how I had enjoyed the film, I had to admit that I had not seen any of it. But by the time we reached home, I had been told most of the story, and the row was already almost forgotten.

Months later the sequel to *Jean de Florette* – a film called *Manon des Sources* – came to the same cinema. We decided about eight o'clock one evening to go, and got to the cinema just after the film began at half past. We were sitting in the forward region, in the last row of what is called the front section of the theatre. We were in a good mood. No question of a huff tonight.

240

After a short while my wife remarked that the opening seemed to be the same as the last one. I thought that perhaps this was a run-through, a kind of reminder of what had taken place in Part One. Or else it was employing the device of beginning and ending the film with the same images, to make some artistic point – like Polanski's *Repulsion*, or the sound of the car crash in Losey's *Accident*. But this was not the case. It was simply that for the benefit of those who had not seen the film before, the cinema was showing *Jean de Florette* today, Wednesday. The sequel *Manon des Sources* would be shown on Thursday, Friday and Saturday. We had made a mistake.

But my wife had enjoyed the film on its first showing, and she generously agreed that we should just sit there again. So the sounds that had formed for me an incomprehensible abstract were now united with their visual images. I was a member of the audience with my companion, and saw nothing of what I had seen so stealthily before.

What I Hate about the News
is
its Definite Article

It's one thing to have wide-angle spectaculars of twelve-rockets-at-a-time whooshing upwards into a dark desert sky, patriotic flag somewhere on screen; it's another to have wide-angle spectaculars of what happens to the conscripts on whom the over eight thousand disintegrating "bomblets" fall from each such salvo. That is taboo. It is also apparently taboo for party conferences in 1991 to discuss what has been – and is – the suffering, destruction and death caused by that "largest bombardment in military history" for which MPs trooped through the Aye lobbies in the time since the previous party conferences met. It really is quite extraordinary. As someone born in 1944, I was reared in the slightly comfortable belief that there was something peculiarly wrong in the behaviour of a German nation whose people apparently never saw – or never bothered to find out – what was happening in the camps during the war. Now I know only too well that my own country can be firing Cruise missiles into foreign cities whilst the topic hanging over Glasgow whilst this is going on, is whether or not Ally McCoist will be on the bench or the park that afternoon. True there has been a deal of self-congratulatory public sympathy, for a convenient while, over the plight of the Kurds; convenient in that for over seventy years no-one cared twopence about their oppression by several countries, and convenient in that the present oppression could be laid at the door of Saddam Hussein. Even more to the point, the forces who had laid waste so much within the country of

Iraq from which the Kurds had fled, could be portrayed to the public at home as angels of mercy.

Every time a report is about to appear describing the horrendous state that Iraq has been left in after the bombing, another He-Wants-To-Take-Over-The-World story swamps the TV channels with another revelation. In fact, as a TV show the "war" and its aftermath has been a great success. Witness when there was talk of the bombing getting under way again recently: the *Sun* even carried the headline *Gulf War II*. They'd got the semiotics spot on. George Bush announced he was thinking of releasing a sequel to the original video. Unfortunately we in Britain can't expect to share every triumph with the Americans: as the American golfer Paul Azinger put it, "We went over and thumped the Iraqis and now we've won the Ryder Cup." Azinger was expressing a truth about how both events have been marketed for domestic consumption. The PR firm which John Wakeham hired to handle Gulf War marketing can take pride in the commodity it persuaded the public to consume.

Of course they did have precedents to guide them. There was the famous TV broadcast – I can't remember if it was BBC or ITV – "A newsflash has this moment arrived from the Malabar front. Our forces in South India have won a glorious victory. I am authorised to say that the action we are now reporting may well bring the war within measurable distance of its end." And there was the daily hate-sessions on TV with The Beast, that Demon from the Deep who is son of Scargill and Khomeini and Gadaffi and Hitler and Benn and Stalin and Red Robbo, all fused into one and stretched from Saudi Arabia to Turkey. But we bombed him! My goodness how we bombed him! Napalm and fuel-air-explosive, multiple rocket launches (the "black rain" as the Iraqi conscripts called it), Cruise Missiles fired from ships, B-52s carpet-bombing Basra, thousand-pounders in the daily routine of two and a half thousand planes. And the helicopters that can hover just over the horizon and fire these rockets that take out the tanks though they don't even know you're there! Kapow! Zap! And then there was the bulldozers and the earth-shakers that could just bury them all alive in their trenches as you charged through the desert! Crrrunch!

A landscape with nothing but bodies and vehicles that looked as if they had been in a tandoori, which is maybe what a fuel-air-explosive bomb is, in its way: but we won. We won. And it's been worth it. Now we can make sure The Beast never uses weapons of mass destruction, he'll never get using the chemical weapons such as we've been making and stockpiling for decades, he won't get any nuclear weapons like the Israelis, he won't get any napalm, or fuel-air-explosive bombs, or Stealth Bombers, or F-111s, or Cruise Missiles, or any other of the things that we need in order to further the Peace Process in the Middle East. So we can sell more and more arms to the Israelis and to those Arab family dictatorships that will keep that good old petrol tank away from the "Empty" sign, and maybe when one day somebody nice to Mr Bush replaces The Beast, we can organise pop concerts the like of which you've never seen to help the poor starving and dying Iraqis who will all officially have become Human Beings again. Then and only then can we maybe think about bombing Iran. Or maybe Syria. Or do you think it will be Cuba? Or finish the Libya job as an hors-d'œuvre? One thing you can be sure of: it will all be part of the Peace Process.

Place the Jury

Today's photograph shows another contest between the Crown and a member of the public at Belfast District Court earlier this year. Conditions fair.

Using a ball-point or fine pen, mark a cross on the picture where you think the jury is. Up to two hundred crosses are allowed per entry, and you may submit as many entries as you like.

Only one 10p Ring-a-Cross stake is allowed per entry, and the Ring-a-Cross double-your-money bonus does not apply to the jackpot.

As no-one has won the Place-the-Jury competition for some years, the jackpot accumulator now stands at £3,450,000.

Employees and their families of the *Belfast Telegraph* are ineligible. The decision of the judges is final.

A Letter on Being Asked to
Contribute to an Anthology

Thanks for your note about the *Poems for Bosnia* anthology. I've found that I very rarely can write poems to request – in fact I'm not prolific at all – but I ought to reply rather than simply be silent.

Also I want to say that in any case I would have difficulty with this one. The *Independent*'s line on Bosnia I consider to be possibly the most nauseating set of sanctimonious guff of all the Press, which is really saying something. These are the people who like all the "qualities" were quite rightly beating the drum not so very long ago to say that no way should Britain or the EEC accede to Germany's demand post haste to recognise their former wartime ally, Croatia: no way, because the civil war there would be bad enough, what with the 300,000 Serbs who would never accept domination by people reclaiming their nationhood who had massacred Serbs by the hundred thousand during the last war; but the conflict would in turn be peanuts again as to what would undoubtedly take place in Bosnia-Herzegovina, where all hell would break loose, etc., etc., etc. But the Germans went ahead, of course, and the Vatican – which has still not recognised Israel – promptly followed suit. After all, the country's last manifestation had been under a fascist Catholic cleric. And what does fascism matter. Then, in that ghastly multiple-way jockeying for influence that goes on amongst the EEC (between France and Germany, between France-Germany and the rest, Britain closest to America or to the EEC, etc.) the EEC and Britain followed Germany and the Vatican's line. It was not "inertia". It was a political decision.

The truth of the matter is that like North Korea, Iraq, the Palestinians, the Libyans, the Syrians, and whichever other country happens to step out of line with Nato or the American-IMF vision of the allowable Present and Future, the rump of Yugoslavia known as Serbia has had to be demonised. That is why it like most of these other countries is under heavy sanctions. It is not that someone like myself looks for the excusing of atrocities committed by Bosnian Serbian soldiers during this civil war. But one has to scan very patiently overseas for any indication that possibly there might be more than one way of looking at what is going on, and that civil war atrocities might not simply be the work of that Bosnian side whose paternal government is regarded as the last remnant of the post-war East-European bloc. The "little Irma" saga and its sequel has been the most palpable and disgusting manipulation of public opinion since the so-called Gulf War. No talks of Mr Major's resignation now, the by-election is a very distant past event. More to the point – and this is the only reason the "airlift" has gone ahead in the first place – the cries of "Bomb the Serbians, Bomb the Serbians" have increased in volume. The airlift began precisely – but of course coincidentally – just as Nato had cleared with the UN that "the means for air-strikes were in place"; a few whole days after America had announced that it was now to be considered a feasibility, and of course Mr Rifkind echoed the words about twelve hours later. And public opinion is now ready. Bomb the Serbians. Think of little Irma.

Well, perhaps one might think of the thousands including many children shot dead or wounded in the West Bank and Gaza Strip, the hospitals there without equipment; one might think of the reports by the Red Cross of the deliberate bombing of Lebanese ambulances, as half a million people had to leave their homes, many to return to a pile of rubble. But these were "terrorist targets", according to Auntie BBC. One might think perhaps of Angola, where cities are under siege for over a year and thousands are presently dying, because an army that Bush backed (and whose advisers are still in place) refuses to accept the result of an internationally monitored election. Two hundred thousand forecast to die in the next couple of months, if sieges aren't lifted. But bugger that, the dying are Blacks and they voted for a Marxist government. One might ask where are the reports of the suffering Somalis, suffering human-rights abuses and death just now under the US occupying forces, according to African Rights monitoring groups. But bugger that too, the grab for Africa is under the guise of humanitarian aid these days, and the ANC have to be monitored in the south. "We" have something called Commanders; "they" have something called "warlords": and that is the word which without a single question has been reiterated by all media since that particular end-to-humanitarian-aid began, in the guise of its facilitation. And what about Iraq, where thousands of children have died as a result of the lack of proper medicines: is none of these children photogenic? Are the children who are dying in Britain because of the cutbacks in the health service – none of them photogenic either? Why, for one instance out of innumerable, have the staff of University College Hospital gone on strike today? Shouldn't they go back to work, screw their outrage at losing fifty casualty beds – and think of little Irma? Are they Communists or what?

Why are private hospitals like the Nuffield in Glasgow laying on beds? Well, at least they've been partly honest, in interview. Partly for the publicity, they say. So Yorkhill Hospital, which used to be the pride of the National Health Service in childcare up here, is reduced these past years to socials, nurses carrying cans round local pubs, adverts in the paper – all for the upkeep of an intensive-care unit for children. And these private hospital bastards are flying sick children in from abroad "doing their bit for Bosnia". As for some kind of in-the-round reporting on Bosnia itself, why does one have to listen to Irish radio to hear that Mostar just now is under siege, the Muslim males have been rounded up south of the river and are being shelled by the Croats, and the women and children are taking shelter underground while the Croats shell what is now the Muslim area of the city? Why does one have to listen to that radio station to hear aid workers say that it is Muslim militia fighting Croat that have largely been responsible for the prevention of aid getting through to the city of Saravejo; why – this morning – that it has been the Muslim militia who are most responsible for firing on those trying to reconnect electricity to the hospitals? If the electricity was reconnected, of course, there would be less need for evacuation.

It is not that Irish radio is some kind of beacon of truth, after all it is the station whose Section 31 outlaws any Sinn Fein speakers or any republicanism considered not suitable to broadcast. But it is refreshing to hear another point of view, albeit from its own interests. It has carried quite a lot of Croat fund-raising, I assume because of the Catholic connection; for the same reason ironically one has been able to hear much more criticism of American foreign policy in South America, because of the Irish worker priests and nuns there. Similarly one has had many reports from the Lebanon criticising Israel, presumably because Irish UN soldiers have been under fire and shelled by the Israelis, blue United Nation bonnets or no. Again, one hears – as last week – lengthy reports on the criticism of Sellafield, eighty thousand complaints about the proposed new development, and a thirty-page protest document from the Irish government. Again, a curious silence this side of the contaminated water.

What is happening in the former Yugoslavia is awful. I can visualise places now under siege quite readily, as I was in Yugoslavia three years ago, stayed at Dubrovnik, had a trip up through Bosnia-Herzegovina; Mostar and Sarajevo I have visited with my family. That specific individuals are being helped, and that ordinary people are responding from ordinary good humanity, I respect. But there is a dreadful manipulation of minds going on, a use of the humanitarian, and of suffering, in the service of the militaristic. That's my belief, and though I haven't yet felt like writing something I would call a poem about it, if I do before the end of the month I'll send it. I'm not saying Don't send help etc., I don't go for that It's-better-that-beggars-get-poorer-they'll-rise-up-the-quicker shite. But it's a complex thing, and I don't believe in demons: unfortunately that is not a position I see in the *Independent*, the *Guardian* or any of the other papers with their resident Max-Hastings-cum-Francis-of-Assisi "frontline" moralisers.

As for the Labour Party. Oh dear. I envisage a cartoon called "Labour's New Policy Documents". It shows our Morningside lawyer-leader wagging his finger over the despatch box and crying "And whatever it is that you're doing, you ought to have been doing it months ago!" But then like yourself I am of a generation now old enough to remember when parliamentary parties actually had different foreign policies – let alone domestic ones. I regard Major, Smith, Ashdown, Clinton etc. all as murderers. That is the truth of the matter, as far as I'm concerned. I am wholly unimpressed with their public expressions of moral outrage. They are not in a position so to do, and neither will their credentials be improved simply because their next projected bout of bombing foreigners is to be by public demand of a cynically whipped-up domestic public.

Forgive me for trying to put my own feelings at length. I assume the sharing of different opinions still possible even in Britain. I enclose the booklet I did at the time of the Gulf bombing. There was a group of Scottish writers that organised an anti-war reading, for which I did the question & answers. Then I was asked to write an essay introducing it, which I found painful even to write, but did so.

Never Shake Thy Gory Locks at Me

a Review of
"Lost Property": an exhibition by
Christian Boltanski
Glasgow Tramway May–June 1994

Dear *Modern Painters*

Here is the transcription of the recording I made when going round the Christian Boltanski *Lost Property* exhibition. When I went on Saturday morning I was the only person there in the huge space apart from two attendants in the corner. I had a small portable dictaphone with me to whisper notes and reactions into, with a view to having a memory stock from which to write a critical article for you later. But I realised on my way home that the finished recording was itself a document which, within the situation of your request to me, could itself be re-created as one of those "transitional objects" — to use D. W. Winnicott's phrase — in which Boltanski seems situationally to specialise.

I have long since tired, in poetry as in other art forms, of that so-conventional representation of the behaviour of "Other" as aid-to-reflection between a supposed "We" of writer and reader. The aesthetic experience offered rests on the agreement that "Other" remains "Other". The reader is flattered into thinking they are gaining access to an experience of universal human value: but this is essentially at the expense of denying full humanity to that "other human" deemed incapable of becoming part of the process.

Amongst several aids-to-reflection the Tramway hand-out suggests "The recent history of European war and mass murder can never be far from our minds." Perhaps it can't. As for the following transcription, I recognise that its language and register is not what you would ordinarily print in the critical pages of your magazine. However, I have hope that it can serve as addition to that store which the Tramway hand-out suggests "offers clues about the people who live here"; and which in its particulars "acts as a poignant reminder of a loss that each of us might have experienced."

Yours sincerely

Tom Leonard

it goes from, eh, purses . . . date found 24/5/93 . . . commercial department, lost property, Waterloo Station . . . no date . . . a whole variety of purses, and I'm not sure if you're supposed to touch them or not . . . suitcases along the bottom, jotters, homework diary, Cathkin High School . . . Another jotter, Brian Keenan 1M2 French, 3/2/23 . . . does Brian Keenan know about this . . . various books, *practical chess endings*, *the pirates of the deep green sea*, by Eric Linklater . . . eh, Burns in . . . eh, I think it's Croatian . . . books very thinly scattered out . . . eh some books in braille . . . eh I wonder if the people know they're here . . . might be better if they did . . . collection of books it looks very . . . eh like a very poor second-hand bookshop . . . very thinly covered, they're trying to make up the most of the space . . . almost running out of shelf-space here with some cheap paperbacks, thinly scattered . . . the iron shelves four to a height eh and about two feet wide . . . eh six paperbacks trying to take up the space before it runs out of space, and now we're going into clothes . . .

the length of the files is about a hundred yards long . . . here we have children's clothes, again very thinly scattered everything . . . nothing piled on top of each other . . . commercial department lost property Waterloo . . . looks like a very cheap jumble sale ranged along some shelves . . . now onto sort of anoraks, there's some children's clothes . . . here's a leather jacket and a coat . . . one of the attendants has been reading a book, she's just come down and put it back . . . wonder if it has not altered the artistic state of the fucking project . . . more stuff, coats, coats . . . one section nine-by-four double-sided, the next shelf fifteen then twelve . . . each by four, doubled . . . now here's some gloves with eh . . . Parkhead Strathclyde buses . . . eh . . . three sets of gloves . . . date 29/11/ 93 . . . some fine bunnits, more gloves and bunnits . . . gloves, again arranged very thinly, more or less one at a time . . . it just looks like a fucking jumble sale that's been stretched through an enormous length of . . . here's keys, oh very good . . . lots of keys . . . very very thinly scattered . . . keys, keyrings, keys, keys keys 1/10/93 date found . . . more keys . . . one would think perhaps they could have . . . eh . . . tried a wee bit more to identify these people . . . more keys . . . just about running out of space now . . . obviously . . . trying to make the most of the length . . .

and now here's some bikes . . . one, two, three, four bikes . . . one of them falling apart, very tasty . . . one a child's, a very small bike . . . eh, looks like the end of the jumble sale we've reached it here eh another eh ancient pairs of trousers . . . McEwan's eh Thistle's thing, it's really quite pathetic . . . now we have a section in which there are . . . [*sigh*] eh . . . three shelves by four in which there is nothing at all . . . now we're onto what looks like wee scraps, there's still more wee bunnits . . . eh, gloves . . . extremely uninteresting . . . more hats, gloves, nothing there really . . . eh, there's no qualitative difference between anything whatsoever . . . here we are back at the keys, to spectacles . . . again, scattered very thinly on the shelves, plenty of space round about them . . . now back to purses, here we're now into purses . . . and handbags, and now some eh . . . rosary beads . . . and lightshades, eh, and then a sheep's skull very like the one that Stephen had in his room, only it's all cleaned up you'd almost think it's the same bloody one . . . eh, wicker baskets, wee bits of bottle wee eh kind of broken-looking watches, none of them looking in very good repair . . . everything looking very dusty . . . cassettes

Jimmy Shand plastic shoes, and now we get the shoes . . .

all aligned, [*sniff*] date found, Bridgeton Cross, child's shoe . . . eh . . . 1/11/93 . . . something slightly obscene about all this . . . more shoes . . . where is the location . . . plenty seem to have come from Waterloo Station . . . from last year, pairs of shoes that are just . . . God help the people that are trying to find them . . . not everything has eh, by any means got a tab on it, hell of a lot of the things once again Waterloo Station . . . with it Waterloo Station how the fuck is it supposed to be about Glasgow . . . eh . . . another Waterloo Station they seem more or less to have got the spectacles all out of Waterloo Station . . . eh seems between March and November . . . February 1993 . . . all arranged very thinly, extremely uninteresting fashion . . . nothing here, eh, one spec case open very tastefully so you can see the holy picture inside . . . now we're back to eh . . . jumpers . . .

Very stoory looking jumpers . . . this is me walking back down the . . . towards the, faraway from the . . . faraway from the entrance eh . . . jumpers jumpers jumpers jumpers . . . quite a nice jumper here . . . 14/2/92 . . . thing came off in my hand . . . more jumpers down to . . . jumpers jumpers, trousers, not very interesting, bits of thing yes everything arranged again, back in the jumble-sale territory . . . [*sigh*] here we are, tops and bottoms, all arranged, he's managed to get four items per shelf at this point, that seems to have been the plan . . . eh, so that's a wee pair of shorts, a T-shirt, and it looks like another T-shirt and a green T-shirt, a shirt, yes, that's shirts and bottoms here . . . mostly . . . eh arranged four at the top though at the bottom it looks as if they've been trying to make the most of it and to fill up the shelf they've arranged two items longways . . . [*sigh*] this, thing is really getting on my tits . . .

so here we are now, now we're at bags . . . there's something obscene about this . . . here's a bag, commercial department lost property 6/9/93 . . . Waterloo Station [*sniff*] . . . ehm . . . this says more about the kind of guy that could arrange this stuff than it does about the people who've lost it . . . though I think it's trying to make it go the other way . . . more bags, just bags 17/9/93 . . . Waterloo Station . . . [*sigh*] oh dear, what a dreary and dismal sight . . . more and more bags, there's something about the way that they're arranged so as to fill up, fill up the space so as to make the exhibition look a damned sight bigger than it is . . . actually Beckett's pile of rubbish with a breath over it would have far more to say than this . . .

a lot of again, lost property department 19/5/92 . . . Waver eh Waterloo Station, so much of it seems to be from Water-loo . . . wonder how much time he actually spent in fucking Glasgow to get his Glasgow things . . . here's Batman, commercial department Waterloo this is bags by the way, bags schoolbags . . . shoulderbags . . . again it's the way they're sort of arranged to take up a lot of room, on the shelves . . . right, that's us up to bags . . .

and now we're down to kitchen utensils . . . and this is me turning round to walk down for the last time . . . eh, at Lane . . . M . . . which is eh . . . there's a couple of, helmets . . . and there's sort of, kitchen items . . . again though very very very sparsely laid out . . . here's some eh, Monklands District Libraries eh, with somebody's actual name . . . 29 —— Street Coatbridge . . . absolutely disgraceful this kind of thing . . . M—— C—— it's her name her junior library card for Monklands District Libraries . . . a girl's name in —— Street in Coatbridge and there's somebody's an identity card for a guy . . . treating people like rubbish, there's something absolutely fascist about this fucking exhibition . . . now here's some hockey sticks eh . . . and eh now this is the towelling department ho ho ho . . . again everything just looks grubby but it's the way it's neatly arranged . . .

now we're into the inevitable umbrellas . . . looks like I think a child's folding car down at the bottom though it might be something else . . . umbrellas all arranged down as if they're trying to fill up the shelves . . . eh there's men's umbrellas,

umbrellas umbrellas umbrellas . . . eh wait a minute till I count
these . . . again when you get to the bottom he's arranged
several umbrellas longways to sort of try and fill up the space
there . . . yes there's a whole umbrella section this inevitably
taking up a lot of the space . . . wait till I count it . . . ehm one
two three four five six seven eight nine ten eleven twelve . . .
twelve by three . . . plus then . . . one two three four five six by
four so that's thirty six plus twenty four . . . whatever that is,
sixty . . . although some of them have just got two on it
arranged longways . . . others have got four . . . eh, one two
three four five you can even have five on them . . . eh . . .

. . . now round in the last straight which is item T . . . and
completely blank for . . . twenty-four . . . totally blank, he
must have ran out, he can't even space them out far
enough . . . ah yes, it's the home straight of umbrellas . . . one
two three four by, one two three four five six is twenty-four
. . . so that was sixty plus twenty-four is eighty-four . . . eh,
where are they from . . . here's one from oh, Milton, pass
Possilpark . . . driver's name and that's the date 31/1/94 . . .
so a fucking umbrella lost in Possil in January can end up in
this fucking place . . . eh [sigh] ah yes he's using, he's really
hitting Glasgow for umbrellas that's an easy one . . . probably
my own fucking umbrella's in here . . . what [?] I left it in a bus
or a taxi . . . bastard, I hope it isn't . . . Parkhead driver, and
the driver on the [?] folding umbrellas . . . I really resist this
fucker . . . Larkfield 21/1/94 gent's umbrella black . . . could
well be mine the cunt . . . eh, no doubt it will give an aesthetic
thrill to the . . .

here we are again . . . anyway . . . so that was, what was I
saying, another one two three four five six by four's another
twenty-four umbrellas . . . things round the back, some of
them just with two on it . . . eh, and now we're getting to a
blind walking stick oh ho ho ho eh . . . twenty-sixth of April a
blind man's walking stick plus crutches, a number of
crutches . . . one two three four five six . . . plus eh one two
three four five six seven, eight nine, ten eleven, twelve thirteen

fourteen . . . fifteen sixteen walking sticks including probably the one that Freddy lost, that he thought some cunt had knocked . . .

Oh we're back to umbrellas for fuck's sake another eh . . . one two three four, another four shelves of umbrellas . . . eh, I must see if I, I think I'll try and end up if I look for my own . . . now we have push-chairs eh . . . so that's one two, you know like shopping trolley ones, one . . . eh one two, three, four . . . five eh . . . then a kind of [?] baby's go-cart, is five by four is twenty . . . eh, and then a lot of wee baby's bottles, one two three one two . . . one two . . . and sort of, bits of bric-à-brac . . . oh and a skateboard and, so on this . . . the whole ethics of it I think are deplorable ehm . . . there's something that really asserts that this is something for . . .

. . . it all has been eh sectioned off with fencing, mesh fencing . . . so it's industrial shelving units, four lines of them . . . eh I don't know what a hundred, hundred feet long . . . hundred yards long rather . . .

I forgot to mention in the section . . . the last section as you turn down . . . where I spotted the television etc, eh, there's sev eh there's four wheelchairs . . . and then some sort of carpets and things . . . and some sleeping bags down the bottom shelf.

NOTES

BBC NEWS 1982

The chatty envoi was a feature of news bulletins for some years. What became eventually John Birt's "mission to inform", i.e. to tell people what to think, with every item having an "expert" explanation, can be traced to the mid-seventies. Then the BBC's news editor, Alan Protheroe, wrote that hitherto society had been a pyramid: if one took away bricks at the bottom it still stood; but now it was like a chimney stack, and therefore – and therefore the BBC News had to "educate" people to appreciate and understand the structure of the society which was under threat of collapse. It was the brief time of the feared Triumph of the Left, when the Labour Party monetarist Dennis Healey almost lost the deputy leadership to the left-wing Tony Benn. All this before the dawn of the saviour Margaret Thatcher.

Barbara Woodhouse was an animal expert who advised breathing up animals' nostrils to gain their confidence.

RANGERS SIGN THE POPE

This temporarily became irrelevant when Graham Souness signed the Catholic player Mo Johnston, albeit apparently to spite Celtic who thought he had signed for them. The words "Traitor's Gate" were painted on the pavement outside the entrance to Ibrox. Then both Souness and Johnston moved on, but at the time of writing (1994) another of Rangers' frequent star signings is understood to be Catholic.

SCOTLAND TODAY

A newsflash for a show written by sundry hands put on by the Wildcat Theatre Company.

MR ENDREWS SPEAKS

The belt was still in use in classrooms in Scotland when this first appeared. The "Kelvinside accent" is more complex than indicated here, I have simply substituted "e" for "a" in certain words to indicate that it's being used throughout.

The west of Scotland is very rigid in its separated Catholic schools. The decline in church-going (or chapel-going, to stick to the tribal terms) has meant that in working-class areas Catholic schools have become mixed, almost by default, since this piece was written. This healthy state of affairs is being remedied through the school closure programme. Teachers must now (from July 1993) have a statement as to their fitness to teach, signed by two Catholic priests. This is bad news for such as the non-Catholic teachers previously transferred into Catholic schools. As the "spare" Catholic schools close, these non-Catholic teachers (and presumably such pupils) can be dumped. "Strathclyde Region: an equal opportunities employer"!

BEER ADVERT

Written for Wildcat Theatre Company.

HAWDYIR SCROTUM: A YOUNG CONSERVATIVE PHILOSOPHER

Written for the revue "Tickly Mince" which also featured work by Liz Lochhead and Alasdair Gray. Eight years after writing, it can at least serve as a reminder of the days when the logical conclusions of monetarism seemed only a topic for satires of the imagination.

Of the song: the eight o'clock walk was the morning walk of people going to be hung. Sidney Weighell was a right-wing trade unionist; Peter Manuel was a murderer who would now be called a serial killer.

ON KNOWING THE DIFFERENCE BETWEEN PREJUDICE, DISCRIMINATION AND OPPRESSION

Published in the *Edinburgh Review*.

MR CHESTY BURNS THE FRIED BREAD

The campaign to tart up Glasgow's image began with the use of the little smiling blob Mr Happy, painted and pasted all over the place, with the motto "Glasgow's Miles Better!" Mr Chesty was written as a little booklet sent to friends at Christmas.

The Burrell Collection has a collection of tapestries as a centrepiece.

THE FIRST NICARAGUAN ARCHBISHOP OF CANTERBURY

For Nicaraguan read Polish, for NUM read Solidarity, etc.

THOUGHT FOR THE DAY, WITH THE REVEREND JIMMY GELMAYEL

Written in response to the massacres at Sabra and Shatila, when Israeli troops under Ariel Sharon let Lebanese Christian Phalangists enter the Palestinian refugee camps, ignoring the gunshot sounds and inevitable consequences.

HOW I BECAME A SOUND POET

A series of international "sound poetry" festivals, often organised in London by Bob Cobbing, took place in the seventies and early eighties. *Cencrastus* requested a feature about the performance and tape-recorder compositions I made for some of these. Stopping work in this area was about the need to move on, not "repression", despite what the article says.

OF WHIGLING PROVOSTS

Written when asked by the *New Statesman* to write something about the impending General Election of 1987.

The complete poem, plus two more of Polin's poems, is in *Radical Renfrew*, published by Polygon.

SOURSCENES FROM LITERARY LIFE

The last line in the second poem is a reference to the Valentine's Day envoi that people used to write on the back of their card-envelopes, NORWICH. Thus "knickers" loses its "k".

A HANDY FORM FOR ARTISTS FOR USE IN CONNECTION WITH THE CITY OF CULTURE

Written in 1989 as an attempt to avoid even having to say anything about the "City of Culture" promotion the following year.

ABLATIVE ABSOLUTE

Some Latin scholars may reject this title on the grounds that "On being seized with" the dry boke is not strictly the past participle passive of a transitive verb; and in any case the construction must never be used if the person or thing involved is either the subject or the object of the verb in the sentence.

The title is poetic licence.

THE MODERATE MEMBER'S MONOLOGUE

Written after Labour's defeat in 1987, and whilst a supposed "listening exercise" was being marketed in which politicians trawled the country asking vetted audiences what it was they would like the politicians to believe. Needless to say everything "predicted" in this piece came to pass; not because of any powers of prophecy of this author, but because not to have seen clearly what was happening required either concentrated powers of stupidity, or perhaps simply an MP's salary.

The EIS is the Educational Institute of Scotland, the teacher's union, which had a partially successful strike which would have been more successful had Labour not decided to distance itself from it in case it spoiled election chances, etc., etc., etc. Other references are to local personages, though it is the principles that count and the names don't matter.

FROM THE FRONT-OF-THE-MOUTH ORAL ACTIVITY MEMBER

A reference to a specific posh-Scottish way of speaking, which seems to have arisen historically as a kind of compensatory guard against the "slovenly" stillness of glottal-stop users' mouth activity, by busily working the lips and the teeth while speaking, in a kind of hyper-crispness. The model for this particular monologue was Michael Hirst.

Lord Young's YTS – Youth Training Scheme – was the first of umpteen blandly named government schemes through which young people were asked to be grateful to be given the chance to do low-paid work, by calling it "training". (See 'BBC News 1982'). The model seems to have been Tom Sawyer giving his pals some "work experience" by getting them to paint his fence.

The scheme was marketed using snappy and sophisticated television commercials.

POUND AND MACDIARMID: FROM A SEVENTIES NOTEBOOK

The addition was added when asked to contribute something to a MacDiarmid centenary celebration.

A NIGHT AT THE PICTURES

This was written when asked to write something for a projected anthology about writers' memories of the cinema. I missed the deadline, but it was first published in the magazine *Gairfish*.

WHAT I HATE ABOUT THE NEWS

This was written when asked to do something for the "What I Hate About . . ." regular feature article of the Saturday *Scotsman*.

PLACE THE JURY

A spoof on the place-the-ball contests in newspapers.

A LETTER ON BEING ASKED TO CONTRIBUTE TO AN ANTHOLOGY

A cyclostyled letter from Ken Smith requested a poem for an anthology, *Klaonica: Poems for Bosnia*, to be put together at speed. The *Independent* had an interest, and Bloodaxe were likely to publish. I did not write the letter with publication in mind, but decided afterwards that it could be a personal contribution to the debate – or lack of it. The "little Irma saga" was a much-publicised airlift of a child to hospital in Britain from Sarajevo.

One year on (December 1994), the proposed bombing of Serbian troops has been repeatedly thwarted because ground troops would suffer retaliation. In looking at all this it is not a question of "siding with the Serbs" – but of questioning why only one side of the matter is relentlessly put forward.

NEVER SHAKE THY GORY LOCKS AT ME

Commissioned partly by Glasgow District Council for May-fest, the exhibition utilised, according to the hand-out, lost property gathered from five lost-property offices in and around Glasgow. Hence the bewilderment at the many lost-property tickets from Waterloo Station.